Copyright © 2025 by Jeanna Swann - When Your Heart Cries
Published by UNITED HOUSE Publishing

All rights reserved. No portion of this book may be reproduced or shared in any form - electronic, printed, photocopied, recording, or by any information storage or retrieval system, without prior written permission from the publisher. The use of short quotations is permitted.

Scripture Quotations taken from the (NASB) New American Standard Bible®, Copyright ©2020 by The Lockman Foundation. Used by permission. All rights reserved. lockman.org.

ISBN - 978-1-952840-63-0

UNITED HOUSE Publishing Clarkston, Michigan
info@unitedhousepublishing.com www.unitedhousepublishing.com

Cover Photo: Jeanna Swann
Photography: Jeramey Rice @jerameyrice
Cover and interior layout: Talitha McGuinness; talitha@unitedhousepublishing.com

Printed in the United States of America 2025 - First Edition

SPECIAL SALES
Most UNITED HOUSE books are available at special quantity discounts when purchased in bulk by corporations, organizations, and special interest groups. For more information, please email orders@unitedhousepublishing.com.

Dedicated to:

To the One who calls me
to know Him more, thank you.

To my family,
especially my husband, Todd,
thank you for all your support.

~Foreword~

I met the author on a warm and sunny day at the church where I served. She came in the door with 2 children, a baby carriage, a diaper bag, and her purse. She was juggling everything to get in the door, but it was obvious she needed help. I opened the door for her, and she entered not only a church building but a journey that has led to the creation of this bible study you hold in your hands. For many years I have observed Jeanna juggle her faith through many challenges, heartache, and uncertainty. The fruit of her commitment to knowing God and His ways was the strength and endurance she received in the challenges and the subsequent health and joy she has been experiencing for many years. In this bible study, Jeanna points you to two profound pathways to peace, healing, counsel, and health. These pathways are the truths of the Scriptures and the author of the Scriptures. This bible study is an investment in your relationship with the Lord and His counsel. The world in which we live is in desperate need of those who, by their values, behaviors, and lifestyle, reflect the goodness and greatness of the Lord Jesus Christ. I highly encourage you to set aside time to focus and engage in this bible study. In doing so, you will reap the benefits of a deeper relationship with the Lord and His faithfulness.

Berry Johnston, Renewal Ministry Associate Pastor
Discovery Church, Orlando, Florida
Berry Johnston has served in several churches in Central Florida for 50 years. He has been a staff pastor at Discovery Church in Orlando, Florida, since 1997, where he has held several roles. He is married and has three children and two grandchildren.

Never read the New Testament
the same way again.

WHEN YOUR HEART CRIES

~Introduction~

What makes other people seem to benefit from reading their Bibles, yet you sit, morning after morning, and nothing sticks? Nothing jumps off the page. Nothing seems relevant to your life. And to be quite honest, the "nothing" just confirms the voice in your head saying, "What difference does it make? How is this helping me?"

Years ago, I sat in that very spot. My husband had just left me and my two very young daughters. I felt aimless, hopeless, hurting, and, quite frankly, worthless. Could this be my life? Although I had been a Christian for years, tried to do what was right, and followed the rules, I wondered where God was in all this.

Perhaps you find yourself in that place right now. You may be wondering where God is in the middle of your challenge. In the middle of your loneliness. In the middle of your grief and shattered dreams. You may feel spiritually "numb," yet long to know God's plan and how to move forward.

I wanted my pain to end, and I needed direction. Psalm 46:10 (NIV) caught my attention. "Be still and know that I am God; I will be exalted among the nations, I will be exalted among the earth!" More than likely, you've seen this verse on t-shirts, bumper stickers, and coffee mugs. As familiar as it may be, this verse gave me the direction my heart was crying for and helped me recognize that "knowing Him" was the key.

This quest to know Him more is now the platform for the study you're holding in your hands.

Could I ask you a favor? You don't know me, but may I ask you to trust me when I say God has the same desire for you and wants you to know Him more than anything?

I believe as we walk through this New Testament study together, you won't just know Him more, but you're going to experience His hand in your daily life. You will hear His voice like never before, and His Word will infuse new life into your spirit.

As a matter of fact, I believe after reading this study, *you will never read the New Testament the same way again.* That's a big claim, isn't it? Yes, it is, but I am confident that as we navigate this unique study method, we'll not just know about Him; we'll know Him more.

Jeanna

Learning To Mine
We All Have "Schema"

A common term used by educators is "schema." Simply put, schema is this: *past information learned or acquired from which we build new knowledge*. Research shows that children with more in-depth schema (learning experiences) have a greater chance of succeeding.

As adults, we carry our schema with us, and as we get older, we build on that knowledge. That's all well and good unless the schema we have is faulty.

In this study, you will combine your schema or your past knowledge with perhaps a new way to read the New Testament. It is going to take trust. It will require a short learning curve, but I believe you will find this method eye-opening in your daily devotions.

This method is known as *mining*.

The technique of mining is to skim the New Testament for a certain word, isolate the word, and then build comprehension around it. We will end each day's study with thoughtful questions like:
- Why did the writer intentionally use that word?
- How does the Greek definition differ from my current understanding?
- What does the Lord want to reveal to me through this newfound understanding as it relates to my life?

To practice this technique, all you will need is a Bible (I'll be using the NASB), a pencil, and your smartphone. (No app required!)

Warning! You may find what you learn challenges your schema, information you believe to be true and accurate. However, mining may reinforce the meaning of scripture you hold dear!

Given our desire to know Him more, we will search the entire New Testament for the word "know." I think you, like me, will be surprised and encouraged by what you find.

Again, the goal of mining is not to enlarge your file of knowledge or provide facts to be regurgitated on demand. We want the Lord, through His Spirit, to give us fresh insight into our lives, comfort us, provide a platform for His voice to be heard, but above all, to know Him more. Mining is about deepening our relationship with Him!

Some of you may find this to be the very thing that will turn your Bible study time into an adventure. Let's get started!

WHEN YOUR HEART CRIES

Oida

WHEN YOUR HEART CRIES

Day 1

*"For the Gentiles eagerly seek all of these things, and your Heavenly Father **knows** that you need all these things.*

But seek first His kingdom and His righteousness, and all these things will be added to you."

Matthew 6:32-33

WHEN YOUR HEART CRIES

Day 1
Let's Do a Little Mining

If we were having coffee together, we would more than likely talk about kids, family, and church. But I wouldn't end our time together without asking, "So, how are you? How are you really? What is your biggest need right now? How can I pray for you?"

Because in my darkest time–during my hardest days–this was the kind of conversation I needed from someone who cared, someone who loved me.

So now I will ask you how you are doing. What is your biggest need right now? How can I pray for you? Even though we may have physical limitations, there are no spiritual limitations. Not one. And until I can hold your hand and pour you a second cup of coffee, I offer this: *Mining*, a Bible study method that gripped my heart and gave me comfort and direction. I want that for you, too.

Thank you in advance for trusting me with this season in your life for the next twenty days. I commit to pray for you until I can take your hand, hug your neck, and pray for you by name.

Let's get started. Turn in your Bible to Matthew 6:32 and fill in the blank.

"For the Gentiles eagerly seek all these things, for your heavenly Father _____ that you need all these things" Matthew 6:32.

Now, let's go mining!

How to Mine:
1.) Grab your phone. Go to your search bar. (I just use Google.)
2.) In the search bar, type in "Matthew 6:32 lexicon." Click Search.
3.) One of the top or first search results will be from Biblehub.com. Click on that search by touching the blue letters.
4.) This will open Matthew 6:32 in the New Testament Greek lexicon, a dictionary. Read the verse again a couple of times from top to bottom in the lexicon.
5.) Notice the blue Strong's numbers assigned to each word.
6.) Click the Strong's number for "knows" (3609a).

The Greek word for "know" in Matthew 6:32 is *"oida,"* which means to see or perceive it.

Please read Matthew 6:32 again, inserting the Greek meaning of "know."

"For the Gentiles eagerly seek all these things, for your heavenly Father knows (oida/ because He has seen it or perceived it) that you need all these things" (Matthew 6:32).

Take a moment to let that sink in.

Here, Jesus is speaking to His disciples. They were early in their relationship with Jesus, yet they hung onto His every word. The message was their Heavenly Father knew what they needed because He had seen it and perceived it. That brings me comfort. How about you?

The word "know" in English doesn't convey this exact meaning, does it? Let's connect our new understanding of "know" and continue in our reading by adding Matthew 6:33.

"For the Gentiles eagerly seek all of these things, and your Heavenly Father knows (oida/ because He has seen it or perceived it) that you need all these things. But seek first His kingdom and His righteousness, and all these things will be added to you" (Matthew 6:32-33).

From the very beginning, Jesus lovingly sought to reframe the thinking of His disciples. He challenged their old "schema," which equated worldly things with God's blessing. With these two verses, Jesus disarmed one of the greatest lies of the enemy.

It is the lie that says, "God isn't interested in your needs, wants, or requests because he has more important things to do." In essence, "You're not important enough."

However, Jesus gives explicit instructions to his new friends. By saying, *"your Heavenly Father knows,"* Jesus reroutes their thinking.
Seek His kingdom first.
Seek His righteousness.
Then, *"all these things"* He knows (because He sees it, or perceives it) will be added to you.

I confess there was a time when I sought the "things" first. I went to the Lord desperately praying for my marriage, as well as many other things. I cried and used my most persuasive words to convince Him to heal my broken relationship. But like the disciples, my greatest need wasn't what I thought.

My greatest need was to desire Him first and to know Him more. It was to seek Him, magnify Him, thank Him, worship Him, and acknowledge Him. When I realized He knew my need before I even bowed my knee, my schema and prior knowledge of the Father changed.

I learned to exalt Him, not my situation.

By mining the word "know," I was able to stop and take a deeper look. This gave the Lord an opportunity to adjust my thinking and build solid truth into my schema, just as He did for the disciples.

I'll take the Spirit of God adjusting my thinking any day over aimless Bible reading. How about you?

Day 2 will bring more mining, but for now, take the nice sharp pencil and your Bible I asked you to grab earlier. Circle the word "know" in Matthew 6:32. In the margin, write *"oida*, to see or perceive it."

We are just beginning this journey, and this aspect can be so exciting as we move through the process. Looking forward to tomorrow!

Something to consider:

Has there ever been a time when the Lord challenged you on a deeply held belief? What prompted it?

_____

_____

_____

_____

Pray with me:
Lord, I am so grateful You know my needs, and I don't have to earn Your blessing. I declare that You are my Heavenly Father, and I place my trust, my knowing, in You again today. Change my heart, Lord, where I have misunderstood You.
In Jesus' Name, Amen

Day 2

*"In the same way the Spirit also helps our weakness; for we do not **know** how to pray as we should, but the Spirit Himself intercedes for us with groanings too deep for words; and He who searches the hearts **knows** what the mind of the Spirit is, because He intercedes for the saints according to the will of God. And we **know** that God causes all things to work together for good to those who love God, to those who are called according to His purpose."*
Romans 8:26-28

WHEN YOUR HEART CRIES

Day 2
Why Mine?

In my quest to "know" Jesus more, I decided a Bible word search would be a great place to start. I quickly realized the Old Testament in Hebrew has over one hundred different definitions and nuances for the word "know." With no theological training, it was a bit daunting for me, but my heart still longed to know more and, most importantly, to know Him more.

Having this desire to learn, I started to skim-read the New Testament, noting each time I found the word "know." Believe it or not, it appears over 530 times. Just like you did on the lesson from Day 1, I went mining by using these steps:
  1.) Circle the word.
  2.) Use your phone to search.
  3.) Study the word in the Greek lexicon.
  4.) Make note of the meaning in the Bible margin.
As a result, I discovered "know" often had a different meaning than my current understanding, my schema.

As a reading teacher, I used skim-reading as a way to teach students to look for details rather than trying to remember facts. The purpose was strictly to find certain details, and once located, they could return to the passage and build meaning around that detail. Through skim-reading, understanding is produced, and with understanding, comprehension is achieved.

Although comprehension is valuable, how can we trust the details found in the Bible with so many different versions? Valid question!

The Bible tells us, *"All scripture is inspired by God and profitable for teaching, for reproof, for correction, for training in righteousness"* (2 Timothy 3:16).

Through centuries of scrutiny, scripture has been tested, proven, and found reliable because God Himself breathed life into it. Every word in scripture, like the word "know," was intentionally placed by God as His love letter to us.

It has been said that if there were one chapter in the whole Bible to memorize, it would be Romans 8. These 39 verses detail a life as heirs with Christ united by His Spirit. It documents a glimpse of our future glory as well as God's everlasting love for us. We will be focusing on Romans 8:26-28, but if you have time, you might find it useful to skim-read Romans 8 in its entirety.

We will continue to mine the word "know" in this chapter, and I'm confident you will find yourself in familiar territory in this passage.

Let's focus on Romans 8:26-28.
Use the "How to Mine" directions from Day 1.

We are in the process of learning, so give yourself some time. Follow the steps carefully. They will become second nature to you soon enough!

Looking at Romans 8:26-28, how often does the word "know" appear?
_____

Using your mining technique, write the Greek word and definition for "know" as it appears in these three verses. _____

_____

In your Bible, circle the word "know" and, once again, place the Greek word in the margin.

Using the definition you just mined, let's read it again.

"In the same way the Spirit also helps our weakness; for we do not know (oida, because we haven't seen it or perceived it) how to pray as we should, but the Spirit Himself intercedes for us with groanings too deep for words; and He who searches the hearts knows (oida, because He has seen it or perceived it) what the mind of the Spirit is, because He intercedes for the saints according to the will of God. And we know (oida, because we have seen it or perceived it) that God causes all things to work together for good to those who love God, to those who are called according to His purpose."
Romans 8:26-28

These verses remind me of a time when my pain was so great that, quite honestly, words escaped me. I prayed all the prayers, yet nothing seemed to change. It felt like God was a million miles away.

Reading these verses now, I can look in the rearview mirror of that painful time and see more clearly how the Spirit of God interceded on my behalf. He, who searched my heart because He had "seen me or perceived me," prayed for me as I cried and grieved when I had nothing left on my own.

Have you ever been there? Have you ever faced a wall of sorrow or hurt, perhaps a challenge that seemed too great for you to handle?

I cannot pretend to know your heart or measure your pain, but this passage tells us of the One who can. Out of His great love for you, He searches your heart and prays for you when you can't even pray for yourself. It's His plan, His *redemptive* plan. Even if circumstances do not change, we can know He is working all things together for our good and His glory because we have seen it or perceived it.

If we hadn't mined this passage, we might have missed the importance and the impact of the word "know" in these verses. That is why we mine.

Something to consider:
Have you ever been in a situation so difficult you didn't know how to pray? How did you move past that point? _____

WHEN YOUR HEART CRIES

_____

_____

_____

Pray with me:
Lord, thank You for knowing my weaknesses and the pain I have endured. Thank You for Your Spirit who lives in me, leading and guiding me into a deeper relationship with You. Help me to trust You as You work all things together for my good.
In Jesus' Name, Amen.

Day 3 will bring even more mining. You are doing some hard work, but it will pay off!

Day 3

*"John answered them saying, 'I baptize in water, but among you stands One whom you do not **know**. It is He who comes after me, the thong of whose sandal I am not worthy to untie.'"*
John 1:26-27

*"The wind blows where it wishes, and you hear the sound of it, but do not **know** where it comes from and where it is going; so is everyone who is born of the Spirit."*
John 3:8

*"Then Jesus again spoke to them (Pharisees) saying, 'I am the Light of the world; he who follows Me will not walk in darkness, but will have the Light of life.' So the Pharisees said to Him, 'You are testifying about Yourself; Your testimony is not true.' Jesus answered and said to them, 'Even if I testify about Myself, My testimony is true, for I know where I came from and where I am going; but you do not **know** where I come from or where I am going.'"*
John 8:12-14

"The Jews then did not believe (it) of him, that he had been blind and had received sight, until they called the parents of the very one who had received his sight, and questioned them saying, 'Is this your son, who you

*say was born blind? Then how does he now see?' His parents answered them and said, 'We **know** that this is our son, and that he was born blind; but how he now sees, we do not **know**; or who opened his eyes, we do not **know**. Ask him; he is of age, he will speak for himself.' His parents said this because they were afraid of the Jews, for the Jews had already agreed that if anyone confessed Him to be Christ, he was to be put out of the synagogue.*
For this reason his parents said, 'He is of age; ask him.'

*So a second time they called the man who had been blind, and said to him, 'Give glory to God, we **know** that this man is a sinner.' He then answered, 'Whether He is a sinner, I do not **know**, one thing I do **know**, that though I was blind, now I see.' So they said to him, 'What did He do to you? How did He open your eyes?' He answered them, 'I told you already and you did not listen; why do you want to hear (it) again?'*

*They reviled him and said, 'You are His disciple, but we are disciples of Moses. We **know** that God has spoken to Moses, but as for this man, we do not **know** where He is from.'*

*The man answered and said to them, 'Well, here is an amazing thing, that you do not **know** where He is from, and (yet) He opened my eyes.'*

*'We **know** that God does not hear sinners, but if anyone is God fearing and does His will, He hears him. Since the beginning of time it has never been heard that anyone opened the eyes of a person born blind.'*

'If this man were not from God, He could do nothing.'

They answered him, 'You were born entirely in sins, and are you teaching us?'

So they put him out."
John 9:18-34

Day 3
John, a Record of the "One Whom Jesus Loved"

What is so special about the book of John? We know John was a fisherman, the son of Zebedee, a brother to James, and one of the disciples. And not just one of the disciples, but he referred to himself as "the one whom Jesus loved." Not a bad self-image, right? Actually, the book of John is the most complete record we have of the gospel of Christ. If you have never read through the entire book, I encourage you to set some time aside to do that.

While mining the book of John for the word "know," we can see it occurs more than one hundred times. I have selected just a few to dig into. The impact of these is astounding.

Using How to Mine from Day 1 as a reference, let's mine John 1:26-27 in your Bible. Take your time to move through the process. It will become easier with practice! We'll begin with a passage about Jesus' cousin, John the Baptist.

> *"John (the Baptist) answered them saying, 'I baptize in water, but among you stands One whom you do not know (oida, because you haven't seen or perceived). It is He who comes after me, the thong of whose sandal I am not worthy to untie.'"*
> John 1:26-27

Once again, circle the word "know" in your Bible and write the Greek word, *oida*, in the margin.

Here, John (the Baptist) begins to fulfill his assignment from God to "prepare the way of the Lord" (Mark 1:3).

Our second passage is John 3:8.
(Refer to the "How to Mine" directions from Day 1 if needed.)

In this verse, Jesus speaks to Nicodemus, a Jewish ruler. Responding to a question about who He really is, Jesus said,

> *"The wind blows where it wishes, and you hear the sound of it, but do not know (oida, because you haven't seen it or perceived it) where it comes from or where it is going; so is everyone who is born of the Spirit."*
> John 3:8

Please take a minute to circle "know" in your Bible, placing the Greek, oida, in the margin.

Jesus appears to be addressing Nicodemus' point, much like a riddle. In reality, Jesus is beginning to establish His spiritual authority here on earth.

Now, let's mine John 8:12-14.

> *"Then Jesus again spoke to them (Pharisees) saying, 'I am the Light of the world; he who follows Me will not walk in darkness, but will have the Light of life.'"*
> John 8:12

With your Greek lexicon open, let's continue mining verses 13-14.

How many times does the word "know" appear? _____
What is the Greek word for "know" in each instance? _____
Let's add the Greek definition while we read John 8:14.

> *"Jesus answered and said to them, 'Even if I testify about Myself, My testimony is true, for I know (oida, because I have seen it or perceived it) where I came from and where I am going; but you do not know (oida,*

*because you haven't seen it or perceived it) where I come from or
where I am going.'"*
John 8:14

No longer using parables, Jesus explicitly states the difference between the Pharisees and Himself. Jesus, God Himself, stood in front of the religious leaders, and they didn't know (*oida*) who He was. (Write "oida" in your Bible margin for this verse.)

Jesus' mission is highlighted in our final passage.

Turn in your Bibles to John 9:18-34. We will mine these verses as well. It is a longer passage with a powerful implication. As you read your Bible, circle the word "know" each time, writing the Greek in the margin. Take an extra minute to add the definition verbally as you read, allowing yourself a few minutes to absorb this very compelling passage.

Did you catch the last five words from this passage?

"So they put him out."

The Jewish leaders could not explain what had happened to this man who had been blind from birth. Suddenly, he could see, and it was a miracle that had never been done before. This was messing with their schema, their prior knowledge, and their *"oida,"* what they had seen or perceived. So what did they do?

They cast him out of their synagogue. They hadn't "seen it or perceived it" before, so they got rid of him.

Have you ever felt like a cast out? In a marriage, by a close, trusted friend, possibly even a parent? It can scar you, but in God's kingdom, He chooses us, the "castouts."

Please hear me when I say this: God is digging a well in you, and that well is called your testimony. All you have been through, and all that has been imposed upon you, is for His purpose, to make you more like Jesus. He is healing you through the power of His Spirit and leading you, guiding you, providing, and protecting you. Just like Jesus saw the blind man, He sees you. He hears your cry for help and will meet you at your greatest point of need.

And just like the blind man, you will share your testimony.

That, my dear friends, is why He came—to heal our brokenness and, more importantly, to save us. He came to heal our blind eyes so we might see Him and know Him as our Savior and Redeemer.

Something to consider:

Reflecting on our study today, which individual do you most identify with? Why?
- John the Baptist, sent to prepare the way?
- Nicodemus, a spiritual man with many questions?
- One of the Pharisees, looking for a way to disprove Jesus' message?
- Or the blind man, desperate for healing?

_____

_____

_____

_____

Pray with me:
Lord, I confess there have been times when I have felt like each one of these people. Please allow me to see You the way I need to. Please allow me to know and trust You like the blind man so my life will bring You glory. In Jesus' Name, Amen.

We can now see how powerful mining just one word can be. The book of John comes alive as we look to the Greek for greater understanding.

But how about you? What part of today's lesson has impacted your heart as the Holy Spirit has spoken to you? Please close out today by journaling what He is speaking to you.

_____

_____

_____

WHEN YOUR HEART CRIES

Day 4

*"Nevertheless **knowing** that a man is not justified by works of the Law but through faith in Christ Jesus, even we have believed in Christ Jesus, so that we may be justified by faith in Christ and not by works of the Law, since by the works of the Law no flesh will be justified."*
Galatians 2:16

"For through the Law I died to the Law, so that I might live to God. I have been crucified with Christ; and it is no longer I who live, but Christ lives in me; and the life which I now live in the flesh I live by faith in the Son of God, who loved me and gave Himself up for me."
Galatians 2:19-20

WHEN YOUR HEART CRIES

Day 4
Which Way Are You Going?

Close to our home is a set of train tracks. I've often pictured myself hopping on the train as it chugs by, dreaming of its destination. On most train tracks, one train travels in one direction and another just a few feet away travels in the opposite direction.

In my heart, I can't help but compare this physical journey to my faith journey. The Apostle Paul provides this familiar passage. It is a narrative of what I hope for in my daily spiritual life.

> *"For through the Law I died to the Law, so that I might live to God. I have been crucified with Christ; and it is no longer I who live, but Christ lives in me; and the life which I now live in the flesh I live by faith in the Son of God, who loved me and gave Himself up for me."*
> Galatians 2:19-20

"I live by faith . . ."
For me, that's the train I want to hop on. That is the direction I want to go. Every minute of every day, I want to be able to say, "I am crucified with Christ; it is no longer I who live but Christ who lives in me."

However, if I am honest, my actions don't always line up with that belief.

It seems Paul was dealing with a group of young believers, both Jews and Gentiles, questioning their spiritual direction. They had put their faith in Jesus for salvation but were pressured by a few false teachers to implement the Jewish custom of circumcision as well. You know, a little Jewish law for good measure! As Paul stepped in to correct this error, he must have thought, "Why are you teaching that? It's the wrong way!"

To clarify Paul's probable objection, I think we need to take a minute and look at Galatians 2:16, an important verse that will give us a better understanding.

I believe we all want to experience "the life I now live . . . I live by faith." But how do we get there?

Let's mine Galatians 2:16 together and look for some answers. This is Paul talking.

> *"Nevertheless knowing (oida) that a man is not justified by works of the Law but through faith in Christ Jesus, even we have believed in Christ Jesus, so that we may be justified by faith in Christ and not by works of the Law, since by the works of the Law no flesh will be justified."*
> Galatians 2:16

This verse might be a mouthful, but while you have your Greek lexicon open, let's define a few words.

We see that "know" in this verse is oida, meaning "to see it or perceive it."

Tip:
On your phone, touch "justified/1344." Look under HELPS Word, beginning with "the believer is made…" to complete the blanks below.

Now, let's look at what 'justified' means. "Made _____, cleared of all _____."

Let's read verse 16 again and personalize it so we read it as though it's talking directly to us.

> *"I know (because I have seen it or perceived it), that I am not justified, (made righteous, cleared of all charges) by works of the law but through faith in Jesus Christ, so that I also believed in Christ Jesus, in order to be justified, (made righteous, cleared of all charges) by faith in Christ, and not by works of the law, because by works of the law, I will not be justified, (made righteous, cleared of all charges)."*

Reading this verse and mining those words in Greek provides a greater depth of His Word, doesn't it? The words "justified," "made righteous," and "cleared of all charges" speak directly to the condition of our hearts.

You see, to live out Galatians 2:19-20 (to be crucified with Christ) and declare it is no longer I who live but Christ in me requires I first live out verse 16.

Let's look at it like this. God created us to desire a relationship with Him. Even though we are a sinful mankind, He provided a way for us to have a relationship with Him through faith in Jesus Christ. At the moment of salvation, we start to ride the "faith train."

But at some point, we can begin to take our lives into our own hands. We begin to live life using our own strengths and abilities. Our desire to be happy, fulfilled, and prosperous overrides our faith journey, and we jump the tracks. We are now riding on the "works train" based on our efforts and resourcefulness. It's the train of self-sufficiency based on us. The "works train," believe it or not, is going in the opposite direction.

Oh, we talk about having faith in our hearts, but we mentally pat ourselves on the back as we tally our good deeds of the day. However, as verse 16 tells us, the works of the law do not justify, ever. Like Paul communicated to those young Christians in Galatia, the law, our efforts, nor our good works, can add anything to the redeeming work of the cross.

Yet there it is, just a few feet away, people on a train moving in the opposite direction. They understand the reality of "being justified," "made righteous," and "cleared of all charges" by Jesus Christ. They live daily in the shadow of the cross. Although they face challenges and even sin, they submit to Christ, living with purpose, joy, and freedom in the midst of whatever life brings. They are "crucified with Christ" daily, yielding all of life to Him. They know the direction they are going.

There was a time in my life when I truly thought God would love me more if I worked harder and proved myself to Him. That belief was just as erroneous as that of the Galatians, who tried to require circumcision. It took a difficult time in my life for the Lord to strip me of a faulty thought process, my schema. Maybe you find yourself there right now. Despite doing everything right, parts of your life lie in shambles or grief.

Today, my friend, I am praying for you. I know the depth of such pain and have felt hopelessness. I have recited before God all of my wonderful works. He, in turn, allowed me to see my life as He saw it, a life desperately needing Him and His redemption.

What I didn't realize was there wasn't one single thing I could do to earn His love. In reality, it was *in my brokenness* I learned to hear Him and to know Him more. I pray that in your grief and sorrow, in your difficult situation, you too will hear Him, know Him, perceive Him, and feel His love like never before.

Something to consider:

As Christians, we have the assurance of our eternal destination. However, if we aren't spiritually conscious, we begin to rely on ourselves to meet our needs. Think of a time when self-sufficiency crept in, and God intervened to get you back on track.

_____

_____

Pray with me:
Lord, I confess there have been times when I have wanted to please You so much that I tied my performance to Your love. I chose to follow You, but then I began to rely on myself. I am sorry. More than anything, I want to walk in Your Word and in the confidence of being solely justified by faith in Jesus. Today, I yield my life to You again.
In Jesus' Name, Amen.

WHEN YOUR HEART CRIES

Day 5

*"**Knowing** that He who raised the Lord Jesus will raise us also with Jesus and will present us with you. For all things are for your sakes, so that the grace which is spreading to more and more people may cause the giving of thanks to abound to the glory of God. Therefore we do not lose heart, but though our outer man is decaying, yet our inner man is being renewed day by day. For momentary, light affliction is producing for us an eternal weight of glory beyond all comparison, while we look not to the things which are seen, but at the things which are not seen; for the things that are seen are temporal, but the things which are not seen are eternal."*
2 Corinthians 4:14-18

WHEN YOUR HEART CRIES

Day 5
Dealing With Sin, Hope to Move Forward

There are two types of sin in this world. There's our own sin, which is disobedience to God, and then there is the sin of others that has been imposed upon us. I've learned both must be dealt with but differently with each.

The Word tells us to repent of our sin. We admit our wrongdoing and change course in our hearts and actions (1 John 1:9). While we are always forgiven, the truth is our own sin can have lasting consequences.

But what about the result of someone else's sin imposed upon us? It can be the harmful and violating actions of another causing great impact on our lives. How do we navigate the turmoil of abuse, abandonment, or grief because of another's actions? What about the tragic loss of life way too soon because of someone else's sin?

This is what I've found. Whether it's our sin or the sin of others, God provides an avenue to move forward.

Years ago, I faced destruction emotionally, financially, physically, and mentally. It was the result of another's actions inflicted upon me. While I wasn't the cause of this injustice, I was certainly left with the carnage and the outcome. In prayer, I cried out for answers and desperately sought the Lord through His Word.

Allow me to share the two principles that helped me greatly during this time.

First, getting God's perspective on my situation was key. My feelings and emotions were raw, my thoughts swirling, but I knew God's Word provided the answer. Long before mining, I landed on these words from Paul. This passage was like gold to me then, and I treasure it even more now.

Let's mine 2 Corinthians 4:14-18. Insert the Greek meaning in the blank.

"Knowing _____ that He who raised the Lord Jesus will raise us also with Jesus and will present us with you. For all things are for your sakes, so that the grace which is spreading to more and more people may cause the giving of thanks to abound to the glory of God. Therefore we do not lose heart, but though our outer man is decaying, yet our inner man is being renewed day by day. For momentary, light affliction is producing for us an eternal weight of glory beyond all comparison, while we look not to the things which are seen, but at the things which are not seen; for the things that are seen are temporal, but the things which are not seen are eternal."
2 Corinthians 4:14-18

What phrase in this passage caught your attention? _____

_____

_____

Let me share several of mine:

"Knowing (oida, because you have seen it or perceived it), *that He who raised up Jesus will also raise you up"* (2 Corinthians 4:14). As I personalize this, I can declare in faith that He will raise me up! This truth brought encouragement to me as I faced very difficult days. Knowing He saw me in my despair and wouldn't leave me there brought such hope. He promised to raise me up. Those words gave me His perspective amid my seemingly hopeless situation.

Did you see this phrase in verse 15? *"His grace which is spreading to more and more people . . ."* Because of what God was doing in my life in the midst of my challenging circumstances, His grace became evident to those around me. That is the mystery of His grace. He freely extends Himself to us when we feel like we have no one. We may not feel or see it, but as His grace is manifested in our lives, others see it, and it *"increases thanksgiving to the glory of God."* Part of getting God's viewpoint is acknowledging and thanking Him for His grace, even if we don't feel or see it at the time. That's our faith in action.

"So we do not lose heart . . ." I remember reading this for the first time in my Bible and thought, "That ship has sailed!" I felt like I had already lost heart, but then I continued to read, *" . . . this momentary affliction is preparing for us [me] an eternal weight of glory"* (2 Corinthians 4:17). All I had ever wanted in my life was to glorify God, and here it was—His perspective on how He was going to do that. I must be honest; I wouldn't have wished this set of circumstances on my worst enemy. Yet, here He was, in the middle of my ugliest days, letting me know He would be glorified in my life.

Paul ends with this statement: *". . . while we look not to the things that are seen but to the things that are unseen. For the things that are seen are temporary, but the things that are unseen are eternal"* (2 Corinthians 4:18). I don't know about you, but those words breathe such promise into my heart. There will be an end to this season. While I know forgiveness, restoration, and healing are ahead, I also know these circumstances will not last forever.

God has a plan for the sin imposed upon us. I sought His perspective and found it in scripture. I hung onto His promises with all my might. In the hard days, when I was tired and worn out, they redirected me and restored me.

A second principle I learned seems almost obvious, but I believe it should be explicitly stated. I learned I needed to invite the Father to invade my circumstances intentionally. Through Christ, we have access to the throne of grace. The Helper stands ready to lead us into all Truth. Leaning into Him–all of Him–was crucial to moving forward. He stands ready for the invitation. His promise to us in 2 Corinthians 4:16 is this: *". . . our inner self is being renewed day by day."* There might be days when you feel as if God is far away, but let me assure you, He is as close as the mention of His name (Ps 34:18-19). If you do nothing else, in faith, call on His name. Your spirit will be renewed.

I am reminded of these words in Isaiah 30:18:

> *"Therefore the Lord longs to be gracious to you, and therefore He waits on high to have compassion on you. For the Lord is a God of justice; how blessed are those who long for Him."*
> Isaiah 30:18

Something to consider:

Given the fact we all sin, would you say you are currently wrestling with a circumstance brought about by your own sin? I realize this is a vulnerable question, but don't let this opportunity pass you by. Dealing with our own sin is imperative to healing and restoration, to knowing God in greater measure. Please take the time to identify a moment, a relationship, or an infraction which you know God wants to deal with once and for all.

_____

_____

_____

What about the sin of someone else, sin imposed upon you? What steps have you taken to deal with the consequences of someone's destructive actions which have affected your life? _____

_____

_____

_____

Praying for you today:
Lord, today I shared a bit of my story that You helped write. Yet, right now I am praying for those who are in the midst of a struggle, the thick of hurt, the uncertainty of tomorrow. Please, Lord, give them the assurance that You gave me through Your Word. Let them know that they are not alone and they are going to make it.
In Jesus' Name, Amen.

WHEN YOUR HEART CRIES

Ginosko

WHEN YOUR HEART CRIES

Day 6

*"Now Peter was sitting outside in the courtyard, and a servant girl came up to him and said, 'You too were with Jesus the Galilean.' But he denied it before them all, saying, 'I do not **know** what you are talking about.' When he had gone out to the gateway, another servant girl saw him, and said to those who were there, 'This man was with Jesus of Nazareth.' And again he denied it with an oath, 'I do not **know** the man.' A little later the bystanders came up and said to Peter, 'Surely you too are one of them, for even the way you talk gives you away.' Then he began to curse and swear, 'I do not **know** the man.' And immediately the rooster crowed. And Peter remembered the word which Jesus had said, 'Before the rooster crows, you will deny me three times.'*
And he went out and wept bitterly."
Matthew 26:69-75

"So when they had finished breakfast, Jesus said to Simon Peter, 'Simon, son of John, do you love Me more than these?'
*He (Peter) said to Him, 'Yes, Lord; You **know** that I love You.'*
He said to him, 'Tend my lambs.'
He said to him again a second time, 'Simon, son of John, do you love Me?'
*He said to Him, 'Yes, Lord, You **know** that I love You.'*
He said to him, 'Shepherd My sheep.'
He said to him the third time, 'Simon, son of John, do you love Me?'
Peter was grieved because He said to him the third time,
'Do you love Me?'
*And he said to Him, 'Lord You **know** all things; You **know** that I love You.'*
Jesus said to him, 'Tend My sheep.'"
John 21:15-17

WHEN YOUR HEART CRIES

Day 6
A Lesson From Peter

I recently viewed a social media post from a mom whose young son was learning the T-ball ropes. She recorded him hitting the ball from the T, but instead of running to first base, he ran straight to second. Despite her yelling directions from the stands and the coaches shouting, "Go to first!" he wouldn't change course. Several attempts were made to get him to return to first base, but in his confusion, he finally collapsed at second base, sobbing.

Yep, he needed a do-over. You know, a second chance to get it right.

You are likely familiar with today's passage if you have been in church for any length of time. Our friend, Peter, provides us with a lesson for our T-ball player as well as many of us. Let's look at what's happened so far for context.

After the Lord's supper with His disciples, Jesus warned them of what was to come. Peter, in particular, boasted of his allegiance to Jesus. However, as the evening progressed, God's plan was revealed. Jesus was arrested, paraded through jeering crowds, brutally attacked, and then presented to Caiaphas, the high priest (Matthew 26:26-68).

Now turn to Matthew 26:69-75 in your Bible, and fill in the blanks. Let's mine these seven verses.

> *"Now Peter was sitting outside in the courtyard, and a servant girl came up to him and said, 'You too were with Jesus the Galilean.' But he denied it before them all, saying, 'I do not _____ what you are talking about.' When he had gone out to the gateway, another servant girl saw him, and said to those who were there, 'This man was with Jesus of Nazareth.' And again he denied it with an oath, 'I do not _____ the man.' A little later the bystanders came up and said to Peter, 'Surely you too are one of them, for even the way you talk gives you away.' Then he began to curse and swear, 'I do not _____ the man.' And immediately the rooster crowed. And Peter remembered the word which Jesus had said, 'Before the rooster crows, you will deny me three times.' And he went out and wept bitterly."*
> Matthew 26:69-75

Please take your time. I hope you see what I see.

Peter, three times, adamantly stated he doesn't know Jesus. He doesn't know–oida–as in he hasn't "seen" Him or "perceived" Him. Peter, for whatever reason, completely denies he has even seen Jesus or perceived Jesus. Wow.

"I do not know (haven't seen or perceived) Him" were Peter's words. That's gotta sting . . . not, "Oh, yeah, I've hung out with Him some," or "I've heard of Him." No, this was a flat-out denial of any kind of history with Jesus, the One who had just served Passover to him, the One who had just washed his feet, the One who had spent years teaching him, painting a picture for his future.

"I don't know Him."

Have you ever regretted a decision, a choice of words, a quick response, or a course of action that played on repeat in your brain? I certainly have, reliving the scene like a movie, over and over. It gets worse the more you replay it.

My guess is, as the rooster crowed, Peter felt like that. I'm sure he replayed his words repeatedly in his head. I'm certain if given the opportunity, he would want a do-over.

Peter's scenario might be different from mine, but the result is the same: feelings of guilt, regret, shame, disbelief, and maybe even self-hatred.

But Peter's story is far from over. Wait until you see what's next.

Find John 21:15-17 in your Bible. Read and circle the word "know" in these verses. Starting with verse 15, open the Greek lexicon and begin reading, filling in the blanks for each verse.

What Greek word is used for "know" in verse 15? _____

What Greek word is used for "know" in verse 16? _____

What Greek word is used for the **first** "know" in verse 17? _____

What Greek word is used for the **second** "know" in verse 17? _____

What is the definition of ginosko? "To know through _____ _____."

> "... and he (Peter) said to Him, 'Lord, you know (oida/because you have seen it or perceived it) all things; You know (ginosko/ through personal experience) that I love You.' Jesus said to him, 'Tend My sheep.'"
> John 21:17

Notice Peter only responded to Jesus with *oida* at first, didn't he?

Oida, not implying any real personal relationship. Was he too ashamed or embarrassed? Did he wonder if there was any relationship left after his denial? Scripture tells us Peter was grieved with intense emotional pain.

But Jesus' response to Peter was just what he needed. It wasn't an "I told you so" or "you failed the test." No, Jesus' response to Peter was on a human level, as a friend and a teacher, reassuring him of their relationship.

Jesus replied, "Tend My sheep . . . follow Me" (John 21:17, 19).

The coolest part of this is Peter's willingness to receive the grace extended to him on that day. His "do-over" had a direct impact on literally millions of lives, even yours.

From that day forward, it is recorded Peter took a leadership role in replacing Judas with Matthias as the 12th disciple (Acts 1:26). It was Peter who, in Acts 2, spoke at Pentecost, where over three thousand souls were added to the church. The book of Acts documents Peter and John as they powerfully shared the gospel of Jesus Christ. The once impulsive Peter, now under the power of the Holy Spirit, witnessed thousands come to faith in Christ, and it was Peter who wrote two books of the New Testament. He was imprisoned and ultimately hung upside down, martyred for his mission to spread the saving good news of Jesus Christ.

That, my friend, is the power of Jesus. That's the power of the cross. It places sinners and rule followers alike on equal footing. We all need a Savior, a Redeemer.

Do you need a "do-over" in your life? Is it relationally, physically, emotionally, or perhaps spiritually? Are you fighting memories or moments from the past that have become part of your identity? It is my prayer you allow our Father, through His Spirit, to redeem you, free you, and bring restoration to your life.

Like Peter, you too can know (*ginosko, through personal experience*) the redeeming, restoring love of God. Only Jesus can free us from emotional pain.

Something to consider:

What was that moment for you, the one on replay? Use as many or as few words to describe it.
It may be painful, shameful, or filled with regret, but I believe it is time to allow the Holy Spirit to strip the power of that event from your life. You may remember it, but it will no longer have accusatory power over you.

___

___

___

"And let the peace of Christ rule in your hearts . . ."
Colossians 3:15

"If the Son sets you free, you will be free indeed."
John 8:36

Pray with me:
Lord, in Jesus' name, bring healing to this moment in our hearts. We confess that we know You, through personal experience, as our Savior and our Redeemer. But we are asking You to remove the impact of those days, that event, that heartache from us. You are our Restorer. We thank You that the enemy can no longer hold it against us.
In Jesus' Name, Amen.

WHEN YOUR HEART CRIES

Day 7

*(Jesus speaking) "'When he puts forth all his own, he goes ahead of them, and the sheep follow him, because they **know** his voice. A stranger they simply will not follow, but will flee from him, because they do not **know** the voice of strangers.' This figure of speech Jesus spoke to them, but they did not understand what those*
things were which He had been saying to them."
John 10:4-6

"I am the good shepherd; the good shepherd lays down His life
for the sheep.
He who is a hired hand, and not a shepherd, who is not the owner of the sheep, sees the wolf coming, and leaves the sheep and flees,
And the wolf snatches them and scatters them.
He flees because he is a hired hand and is not concerned
about the sheep.
John 10:11-13

WHEN YOUR HEART CRIES

Day 7
Sometimes You Have to Spell It Out

You've been mining the New Testament for the word "know" for several days, understanding the Greek meaning to be *oida*, to see or perceive it. However, yesterday, I threw you a curveball by introducing another Greek meaning for the word "know," which is *ginosko*, to know through personal experience.

This is the joy of mining. It allows the Lord to reveal Himself in a new way by looking at scripture a bit deeper, and I hope this process is doing the same for you.

Our passage today might be a familiar one, John 10:1-17. Using your Bible, phone, and mining technique, let's skim through these verses. Continue to circle the word "know" and place its Greek meaning in the margin of your Bible.

Now that you've finished mining let's break this passage down. Jesus, who had just healed a man blind from birth, is speaking to the same group of unbelieving, defiant Jews. In verses 10:1-6, He begins teaching about a shepherd.

These Jews were undoubtedly familiar with the concept of a shepherd. They could recall Psalm 23, "The Lord is my shepherd." They certainly were acquainted with Isaiah 40:1-11 and Jeremiah 23:1-4. Most likely, they'd studied Ezekiel 34, as well as the days of Moses, recorded in Isaiah 63:11.

These passages were part of the fabric of their faith.

Teaching about a spiritual shepherd shouldn't have surprised them. Jesus spoke of the thief and the robber who stole the sheep for selfish gain and the gatekeeper who protected the sheep at night. He told of a shepherd who called each sheep by name.

Jesus shared this with the group, saying, *"When he puts forth all his own, he goes ahead of them, and the sheep follow him, because they know (oida, have seen or perceived) his voice."* (John 10:4). Yet regarding a stranger, Jesus said, *"A stranger they simply will not follow, but will flee from him, because they do not know (oida, haven't seen or perceived) the voice of strangers"* (John 10:5).

This seems pretty clear-cut, doesn't it? But the Jews didn't get it. They didn't understand what He was saying (v6). The reason for this, I believe, lies in the passage. Search John 10:6 in the Lexicon on your phone. Look specifically at the word "understand."

What is the Greek for "understand" in this verse? _____

Ginosko, to know through personal experience. Yes, through personal experience, and they simply didn't have that.

They had only *heard* about God being their shepherd. Their years of teaching in the temple should have led them to this moment of realization that the Good Shepherd was standing right in front of them. Yet they only knew *oida*, a knowledge from only seeing or perceiving.

So what did Jesus do?
He spelled it out for them.

"I am the Good Shepherd . . ." (John 10:11).

In John 10:12-13, Jesus explicitly details the difference between a hired hand shepherd and a true shepherd.

"He who is a hired hand, and not a shepherd, who is not the owner of the sheep, sees the wolf coming, and leaves the sheep and flees, and the wolf snatches them and scatters them. He flees because he is a hired hand and is not concerned about the sheep."
John 10:12-13

In essence, a hired hand cares nothing for the sheep. There is no personal relationship with them. A hired hand flees when danger appears in the form of a hungry wolf or thief. He takes off when danger comes because he's not about to risk his life for a bunch of sheep. He doesn't love those sheep or know them by name. He is not emotionally invested in them or their welfare. He's a placeholder. In many cases, a worthless placeholder.

To be quite honest, the Jews were accustomed to faulty, worthless placeholders. The Old Testament was full of them, priests and kings who had failed God's people miserably. But God never backed away from His plan.

In *They Smell Like Sheep*, Dr. Anderson wrote:
> "God pictured his prophets, priests, and kings as shepherds.
> God expected the prophets and priests of Israel to shepherd his people, but they often failed miserably at their task. Although many did not live up to their role as shepherd, God came back again and again to the idea that the leaders of his people were shepherds, even though some were bad."[1]

While many Jews didn't understand *"ginosko,"* God never wavered. While kings and priests failed at shepherding their sheep, God was steadfast. He never lowered the bar to meet their willingness or understanding. Centuries before these Jews ever even breathed air into their lungs, His Word and His plan stood fast.

The Good Shepherd promised throughout the Old Testament was delivered with the birth of Jesus Christ in the New Testament.

You see, a real shepherd–a Good Shepherd–knows (*ginosko, through personal experience*) His sheep. And here's the kicker: His sheep know (*ginosko*) Him.

Look at John 10:14-15.

> *"I (Jesus) am the good shepherd. I know (ginosko/ through personal experience) My own and My own know (ginosko/ through personal experience) Me, even as the Father knows (ginosko/ through personal experience) Me and I know (ginosko/ through personal experience) the Father; and I lay down my life for the sheep."*

A real shepherd loves and protects his sheep no matter the cost. He stands ready to defend them when danger lurks, and out of love, He always pursues the one who wanders.

That is not *oida*; that is *ginosko*. However, the Jews never understood and tried to stone Him.

But here is the amazing part: the story of the Good Shepherd continues today. Knowing the Good Shepherd, *ginosko*, through personal experience makes all the difference. You see, the question isn't whether or not the Good Shepherd knows you. The real question, my friend, is whether or not you know (*ginosko*) the Good Shepherd. That is the eternal question.

You may have had people in your life who were called to shepherd and care for you but failed miserably. I certainly have. But the Good Shepherd never fails, and He invites us to know (*ginosko*) Him. Placing our faith and trust in Jesus is *ginosko*, and the beginning of a personal relationship with Him.

Let's close today's study by reflecting on David's prayer, Psalm 23.

> *The Lord is my shepherd; I shall not want.*
> *He makes me lie down in green pastures. He leads me beside still waters.*
> *He restores my soul.*
> *He leads me in paths of righteousness for his name's sake.*

> *Even though I walk through the valley of the shadow of death, I will fear no evil,*
> *For you are with me; your rod and your staff, they comfort me.*

You prepare a table before me in the presence of my enemies;
You anoint my head with oil; my cup overflows.
Surely goodness and mercy shall follow me all the days of my life,
and I shall dwell in the house of the Lord forever.

This is a dialogue of one who knows (*ginosko*) his Shepherd.
Could you pray this prayer as one who knows his Shepherd?

Something to consider:

Focusing on Psalm 23, take a minute to underline a phrase that speaks to your greatest need right now. Prayerfully ask the Lord to reveal Himself to you concerning your specific need.
He loves you.

Take a moment to journal what the Lord has shown you today.

_____

_____

_____

Pray with me:
Lord, I am so grateful that I can call You my Shepherd. You know me in a personal way and You desire for me to know You personally. Show me what it means to know You more, and to experience Your love in my life. Let me hear Your voice and walk in Your ways all the days of my life. In Jesus' Name, Amen.

WHEN YOUR HEART CRIES

Day 8

*"Now before the Feast of the Passover, Jesus **knowing** that His hour had come that He would depart from this world to the Father, having loved His own who were in the world, He loved them to the end."*
John 13:1

"'Lord, do you wash my feet?' Jesus answered and said to him, 'What I do you do not realize now, but you will understand hereafter.'"
John 13:6b-7

*"A new commandment I give to you, that you love one another, even as I have loved you, that you also love one another. By this all men will **know** that you are my disciples, if you have love for one another."*
John 13:34-35

*"'If I go and prepare a place for you, I will come again and receive you to Myself, that where I am, you may be also. And you **know** the way where I am going.' Thomas said to him, 'Lord, we do not **know** where you are going, how can we **know** the way?' Jesus said to him, 'I am the way, and the truth, and the life; no one comes to the Father but through me. If you had **known** Me, you would have **known** My Father also; from now on you **know** Him and have seen Him.'"*
John 14:3-7

*"Jesus spoke these things, and lifting up His eyes to heaven, He said, 'Father, the hour has come; glorify your Son, that the Son may glorify you . . . that to all whom You have given Him, He may give eternal life. And this is eternal life, that they **know** You.'"*
John 17:1-3

WHEN YOUR HEART CRIES

Day 8
And This is Eternal Life

I was hired to demonstrate an adjustable pillow on a national shopping channel in front of millions of viewers. While it was live TV, almost every word I said had been scripted and approved by the network. What I learned is people can make some pretty wild claims and then are unable to deliver. The network knew in order to maintain integrity for its future, it would only make promises it could keep.

Jesus, in John 17:3, makes such a claim. "This is eternal life, that they may know You . . ."

Jesus' statement is emphatic, isn't it? But what if I told you His assertion was part of a much bigger story?

John 13-17 is a unique group of chapters that culminate with Jesus' statement and is referred to as the Farewell Discourse. Take a few minutes to skim-read these chapters and mine the word "know." You'll find both *oida* and *ginosko*.

Jesus' declaration of eternal life seems so simple, yet let's look at a *timeline* of what led up to His claim.

"Jesus knowing that His hour had come that He would depart out of this world" (John 13:1) signaled events that started to unfold.
Jesus secures a large upper room to meet one final time with His disciples

(Luke 22:7-13).

Together, they had Passover. Jesus, however, abstained from eating (Luke 22:14-18).

Jesus took the role of a servant by washing the feet of His disciples (John 13). The exchange between Him and Peter went something like this:

"'Lord, do you wash my feet?' Jesus answered and said to him, 'What I do you do not realize now, but you will understand hereafter'" (John 13:6-7).

Using our Bibles, let's mine John 13:6-7. Look specifically at the words "realize" and "understand" in your lexicon.

What Greek word do you find for "realize?" _____

What Greek word do you find for "understand?" _____

Let's read those verses again using the Greek definitions.

"'Lord, do you wash my feet?' Jesus answered and said to him, 'What I do you do not realize (oida/haven't seen or perceived it) now, but you will understand (ginosko/through personal experience) hereafter.'"
John 13:6-7

This passage gives us a glimpse of the upper room: Jesus and His carefully chosen dialogue, the disciples, and a clock that's ticking . . . Jesus knew His hour had come.

John continues to memorialize the events of the night as they unfold:

Jesus announces one of them will betray Him. (John 13:21-30)
Judas leaves.

Knowing His time is short, Jesus desperately pours into the remaining eleven. He says, *"A new commandment I give to you, that you love one another, even as I have loved you, that you also love one another. By this all men will know that you are my disciples, if you have love for one another"* (John 13:34-35).

Take a moment to mine the word "know" in these two verses, John 13:34-35.

What Greek word for "know" is used? _____

"By this all people will know (ginosko/through personal experience) that you are my disciples, if you have love for one another" (John 13:35).

I believe this statement by Jesus provides a clear picture of His expectations for us as Christians.

Now, time is fleeting; emotions are swirling as Jesus predicts Peter's denial. (John 13:38)

Jesus, no doubt aware of the brevity of these last moments, provides a roadmap for His disciples, transitioning their thinking from their current physical realm to a spiritual one.

Using your Bible, mine John 14:3- 7 with me, and notice Jesus' word choice.

> *"'If I go and prepare a place for you, I will come again and receive you to Myself, that where I am, you may be also. And you know (oida, because you've seen it or perceived it) the way where I am going.' Thomas said to him, 'Lord, we do not know (oida, haven't seen it or perceived it) where you are going, how can we know (oida, see it or perceive it) the way?' Jesus said to him, 'I am the way, and the truth, and the life; no one comes to the Father but through me. If you had known (ginosko, through personal experience) Me, you would have known (oida, because you would have seen or perceived) My Father also; from now on you know (ginosko, through personal experience) Him and have seen Him.'"*
> John 14:3-7

That's a lot to absorb, isn't it? I especially love, ". . . from now on you know(*ginosko*) Him."

Jesus knows He must continue. He knows His time has come. So what does He do? He promises them the Holy Spirit. (John 14:15-31) And with that, He calls His disciples to rise, leave the upper room, and proceed to the Mount of Olives together.

The clock is ticking, but Jesus continues to earnestly teach these men He loves so much.
"I am the true vine, and My Father is the vinedresser" (John 15:1).
"I am the vine, you are the branches; he who abides in Me and I in him, he bears much fruit, for apart from Me you can do nothing" (John 15:5).

So much wisdom is imparted to them, yet time is slipping away.

Jesus gives insight into the work of the Holy Spirit and how He has overcome the world.
(John 16)

But again, the clock, *"... the hour is coming; indeed it has come"* (John 16:32).

Then, here it is.
"Jesus spoke these things, and lifting up His eyes to heaven, He said, 'Father, the hour has come; glorify your Son, that the Son may glorify you ... that to all whom You have given Him, He may give eternal life. And this is eternal life, that they know You (Father).'" (John 17:1-3).

"And this is eternal life, that they *know (ginosko)* You," through personal experience. It comes down to this; nothing else matters. All eternity has led up to this moment and the events that will follow. Yet, Jesus sums it up in this one statement. Only He has the authority to make this emphatic claim.

This is eternal life ... that they know you through personal experience.

As Jesus prayed in those final moments, He prayed for Himself, His disciples, and, yes, for us. John 17 narrates the intimate words Jesus whispered to His Father, knowing full well that things would get worse before they got better. Yet, we hear His heart's cry that we would know the Father and have eternal life.

Something to consider:

So many times, I've been guilty of reading through John 13-17, remembering only bits and pieces of Bible stories, yet I have never really thought of Jesus making the most of those last few hours as the clock ticked away. He wanted no stone left unturned and nothing left unsaid. How has mining these chapters impacted your view of Jesus' last few hours with the men He loved so much? Is there a time in your life when you can confidently state you moved from knowing (*oida*) Jesus to knowing (*ginosko*) Jesus? That is the eternal question we must all answer.

_____

_____

_____

Pray with me:
Father, I am so thankful for this record of Jesus and His final hours before He gave His life for me. What a sacrifice. And now, more than anything, I want to know You more. I don't just want to know about You; I want to know You experientially on a daily basis. I realize that begins with giving my life to You and trusting You to be my Lord and Savior. But I also want to grow in my relationship with You. Show me how to do that today. In Jesus' Name, Amen.

WHEN YOUR HEART CRIES

Day 9

*"We **know** love by this, that He laid down His life for us, and we ought to lay down our lives for the brethren."*
1 John 3:16

*"We will **know** by this that we are of the truth, and will reassure our heart before Him; in whatever our heart condemns us, God is greater than our heart, and **knows** all things. Beloved, if our heart does not condemn us, we have confidence before God; and whatever we ask we receive from Him, because we keep his commandments and do the things that are pleasing in His sight. This is His commandment, that we believe in the name of His Son Jesus Christ and love one another, just as He commanded us. The one who keeps His commandments abides in Him, and He in him. We **know** by this that He abides in us, by the Spirit whom He has given us."*
1 John 3:19-24

WHEN YOUR HEART CRIES

Day 9
Get To the Heart of It

As we have mined the New Testament for the word "know," some passages hit me harder than others. Today's focus scripture is just that.

I confess that I struggle with a condemning heart. I don't know if it's a result of years as a failed rule follower, marital neglect and abuse, or just a deep need to be good enough. But I do know, (*ginosko*), a condemning heart. If you, like me, have experienced seasons of something similar, today's lesson is for both of us.

Together, let's mine 1 John 3:16, 19-24. Fill in the blanks with the Greek word.

"We know _____ love by this, that He laid down His life for us, and we ought to lay down our lives for the brethren" (1 John 3:16).

"We will know_____ by this that we are of the truth, and will reassure our heart before Him; in whatever our heart condemns us, God is greater than our heart, and knows _____ all things. Beloved, if our heart does not condemn us, we have confidence before God; and whatever we ask we receive from Him, because we keep His commandments and do the things that are pleasing in His sight. This is His commandment, that we believe in the name of His Son Jesus Christ and love one another, just as He commanded us. The one who keeps His commandments abides in Him, and He in him. We know _____ by this that He abides in us, by the Spirit whom He has given us" (1 John 3:19-24).

Take a minute to re-read those verses interjecting the Greek meaning of the word "know." As you read, however, underline any phrase in these verses that gives you pause in your spirit, and take a moment to reflect on what the Holy Spirit may be saying to you.

First, let's acknowledge the meaning of "know" in each occurrence. It is *ginosko*, to know through personal experience. There is no *oida* within this passage. John's writing specifies he is speaking to believers who have *ginosko* with Christ, "by the Spirit whom He has given us."

Next, search 1 John 3:19 using the Lexicon on your phone. Notice all the occurrences of the word "heart" in verses 19-21. "Heart" is mentioned in each of these verses, all with the same meaning. The definition in each instance is mind-blowing.

Heart–*kardia*–means the mind, will, and inner self (our emotions). Each time the word "heart" is used here, it refers to our mind, will, and emotions, certainly not the organ that pumps blood through our physical bodies.

Let's look together:
- 1 John 3:19: *"We will know by this that we are of the truth and (will) reassure our heart (kardia: our mind, will and emotions) before Him."*
- 1 John 3:20a: *"In whatever our heart (kardia: our mind, will and emotions) condemns us . . . "*
- 1 John 3:20b: *" . . . God is greater than our heart . . ."* (kardia: our mind, will, and emotions)
- 1 John 3:21: *" . . . if our heart (kardia: our mind, will and emotions) does not condemn us, we have confidence before God."*

Maybe you, like me, need to take a minute and let those verses sink in.

Clearly, John is separating our souls–our own individual hearts (our mind, will, and emotions)–from the spirit part of us where the Holy Spirit is sealed. Any condemnation we feel originates in our heart, *kardia*. It is not from the Lord.

But if God doesn't condemn us, and we are Christians, why do we struggle with very real feelings of condemnation? They can make us feel like we aren't good enough or need to do more.

Hebrews 4:12 provides an answer:
"For the word of God is living and active, and sharper than any two-edged sword, and piercing as far as the division of soul and spirit, of both joints and marrow, and able to judge the thoughts and intentions of the heart (kardia: mind, will and emotions)."

That verse is saying we must appeal to our own hearts using God's Word. It is the Word, through the power of the Holy Spirit, that transforms our condemning heart. I don't want to communicate this process as formulaic. It is not. We can have deeply held beliefs, grief, or even trauma, which often needs assistance and support. But our experiences cannot define the Word of God. It is the Word of God that should *redefine* our experiences.

Let me give an illustration.

I had a beautiful red cotton blouse with a white collar. Then I washed it, and the red dye bled onto the white collar. With just a single washing, one color impacted the other. At first, there was just a small amount of red bleeding onto the white, but as I washed it again, the white color became unrecognizable. It was completely covered–transformed.

That is a picture of what happens when we submit our hearts, *kardia*, to the Lord. His Spirit that is sealed in us "bleeds" into our hearts, our kardia (mind, will, and emotions). As we pray and meditate on His Word, He changes and heals us. He reframes our thoughts as they relate to our lives and transforms us, bringing His life–His heart–into our lives and our hearts.

> "He restores my soul."
> Psalm 23:3a

Our confidence isn't from ourselves.
"Beloved, if our heart does not condemn us, we have confidence before God; and whatever we ask we receive from Him, because we keep His commandments and do the things that are pleasing in His sight . . . we

know (ginosko) by this that He abides in us . . ."
1 John 3:21-22, 24

Something to consider:

Clearly, it is God's desire for us to be free from a condemning heart. Is there an area of your heart, possibly an experience or belief, that keeps you with a condemning heart? What scripture can you use to reframe that instance? Let's remember it's Truth that transforms our hearts and minds. I am praying for us both as we submit our condemning hearts to Him.

_____

_____

_____

Pray with me:
Lord, I submit my condemning heart to Your Word:

"There is therefore now no condemnation for those who are in Christ Jesus."
Romans 8:1

"Who is the one who condemns? Christ Jesus is He who died, yes, rather who was raised, who is at the right hand of God, who also intercedes for us (me)."
Romans 8:34

"Now to Him who is able to keep you (me) from stumbling, and to make you (me) stand in the presence of His glory blameless with great joy, to the only God, our Savior, through Jesus Christ our Lord, be glory, majesty, dominion, and authority, before all time and now and forever."
Jude 1:24-25

In Jesus' Name, Amen.

Day 10

(Paul writes) "Although I myself might have confidence even in the flesh.
If anyone else has a mind to put confidence in the flesh, I far more;
Circumcised the eighth day, of the nation of Israel, of the tribe of Benjamin,
a Hebrew of Hebrews; as to the Law, a Pharisee;
as to zeal, a persecutor of the church; as to righteousness which is in the Law, found blameless.
But whatever things were gain to me, those things I have counted as loss for the sake of Christ.
*More than that, I count all things to be loss in view of the surpassing value of **knowing** Christ Jesus my Lord, for whom I have suffered the loss of all things, and count them but rubbish so that I may gain Christ,*
And may be found in Him, not having a righteousness of my own derived from the Law,
But that which is through faith in Christ, the righteousness which comes from God on the basis of faith,
*That I may **know** Him*
And the power of His resurrection and the fellowship of His sufferings, Being comforted in His death;
In order that I may attain to the resurrection from the dead."
Philippians 3:4-11

WHEN YOUR HEART CRIES

Day 10
Close the Door and Press On

Years ago, I attended a worship leaders' conference. It was my hope to learn and improve in that area of leadership. While it was an amazing conference, to this day, I only remember one interchange.

A prominent, well-respected worship leader (I'll call him Sam) led a discussion with a small group of us. After his teaching, he opened the floor for questions. I recall the high level of excitement and expectancy as different people asked for his thoughts about various worship topics. The very last question was posed by a man, well-dressed in a sharp, white linen suit. As he stood, he said something like this: "Sam, you lead worship in one of the largest churches in the country, you've won many awards in both secular and Christian venues, you are highly respected everywhere, and your music is recorded live and automatically distributed throughout the world. You are clearly in high demand. With all of your accomplishments, what is your greatest fear?"

You could have heard a pin drop as Sam drew a breath to answer. His response was simply this: "My greatest fear is that I will begin to believe all of the wonderful things people say about me."

His statement took the wind out of the room. He identified one of the greatest threats to a Christian's life: our human desire to feel important and self-righteousness. Sam knew firsthand the truth of Paul's words in Philippians 3:4-11.

Using your Bible, let's explore and mine Philippians 3:4-11 together, looking for the word "know."

What attributes in verses 5-6 are part of Paul's heritage?
_____

How does he view his history now? (v. 7)
_____

Philippians 3:8 tells us why.
"More than that, I count all things to be loss in view of the surpassing value of knowing Christ Jesus my Lord . . ."
Using your Greek lexicon, record what "knowing" means in this verse.
_____

What word does Paul use in verse 8 to describe what he lost?
_____

He exchanged all of these to gain what? (v. 8)
_____

Let's continue to look at verses 9-10 together.
*". . . and may be found in Him, not having a righteousness of my own derived from the Law, but that which is through faith in Christ, the righteousness which comes from God on the basis of faith—**that I may know Him** and the power of His resurrection, and the fellowship of his sufferings, being conformed to His death"* (Phillippians 3:9-10).

Paul has established that even though he has ample reason to think highly of himself, his righteousness is not his own. His background could have been in the "Who's Who" of Jewish history. He hit every mark. It was a part of who he was, his very identity.

That is until Jesus.

Let's look again at what Paul writes. *". . . Not having a righteousness of my own . . . but that which is through faith in Christ . . . that I may know Him . . . "* (Phillippians 3:9-10).

Knowing Jesus Christ through personal experience gave Paul a new identity. He closed the door on his own self-righteousness and the desire to feel important. He allowed Jesus to exchange his identity based on himself for an identity founded in Christ.

My friend, I am certainly aware your life experience may contain other things. Your identity may hold regret, sorrow, humiliation, or lingering grief. It may not be a trophy case of worldly accomplishments, but you're not alone. There isn't a person reading this today who doesn't know those times. But here is the good news, the very best news:

Jesus' righteousness is the great exchange for everyone who believes.

He takes our past, whether difficult or glorious and provides a new identity solely based on Him. Just like Jesus walked into Paul's life, He has walked into yours and mine. In fact, take encouragement from Paul's self-assessment.

"It is a trustworthy statement deserving full acceptance, that Christ Jesus came into the world to save sinners, of whom I am the foremost."
1 Timothy 1:15

Paul saw himself as the foremost of all sinners. Yet today, we speak about Paul for one reason and one reason only: Paul was willing to close the door on everything that defined him. The identity that formerly provided him with worth, power, and privilege no longer had value. He put it all aside and counted it worthless compared to knowing (*ginosko*) Jesus Christ.

But what do we do now? Our faith is in Christ; we've closed the door on all those things we once believed secured our righteousness.

Paul shares the next step. *" . . . I press on so that I may lay hold of that for which also I was laid hold of by Christ Jesus . . . I press on toward the goal for the prize of the upward call of God in Christ Jesus"* (Philippians 3:12,14).

I press on. I pursue Him with a whole heart. I close the door once and for all on my past and press on.

Something to consider:

As you have worked through our study today, has the Lord identified anything that still defines you other than Him? A job, degree, moments of success? What about a failure, a moment of regret, a sorrow you bear daily? _____

_____

Are you at a place where you can close the door once and for all to anything that defines your worth and value apart from Jesus? The very fact that you are doing this study confirms your desire for your worth and value to rest solely in Christ.

Pray with me:
Lord, with all my heart, I want You and You alone to decide my worth, my value, and my identity. I count all things as loss to the greatness of knowing You. I close the door on what the world calls good and lay it at Your feet. I take on Your righteousness completely from this time forward. I choose to press on, as Your chosen, Your called, to press on in You. In Jesus' Name, Amen.

WHEN YOUR HEART CRIES

WHEN YOUR HEART CRIES

Epiginosko

WHEN YOUR HEART CRIES

Day 11

*"Beware of the false prophets, who come to you in sheep's clothing but inwardly are ravenous wolves. You will **know** them by their fruits. Grapes are not gathered from thornbushes, nor figs from thistles, are they? So, every good tree bears good fruit, but the bad tree bears bad fruit. A good tree cannot produce bad fruit, nor can a bad tree produce good fruit. Every tree that does not bear good fruit is cut down and thrown into the fire. So then,*
*you will **know** them by their fruits.*
*Not everyone who says to me, 'Lord, Lord,' will enter the kingdom of heaven, but he who does the will of my Father who is in heaven. Many will say to Me on that day, 'Lord, Lord, did we not prophesy in Your name, and in Your name cast out demons, and in Your name perform many miracles?' And then will I declare to them, '**I never knew you**; depart from me, you who practice lawlessness.'"*
Matthew 7:15-23

WHEN YOUR HEART CRIES

Day 11
To Know Exactly Through Direct Relationship

Have you ever taken a bite of a cookie only to find a different hidden flavor inside? It's an unexpected surprise, isn't it? Well, as I studied "know" in the New Testament, I found a third derivative that, while not used with great frequency, holds a very special place in our study.

It is the Greek word *epiginosko*, which means "to know exactly through a direct relationship." I think you will be surprised by the use of *epiginosko*, and the impact it will have on some familiar passages.

First, let's touch on a bit of grammar. *Epiginosko* begins with the prefix *epi*. *Epi* elevates the meaning of the word it's attached to, in this case, *ginosko*. In essence, it intensifies the word *ginosko*. *Epiginosko* is used over forty times in the New Testament and will be found in your Bible using several English words: know, recognize, perceive, or understand.

Now, in context, let's mine Matthew 7:15-23. Once again, using your phone, open the Greek lexicon to these verses. Please take the time to circle the word "know" or, in this case, any word used for *epiginosko*, in your Bible. Note the meaning in the margin, too.

In Matthew 7:15-23, Jesus teaches His disciples and the crowds of followers. Matthew, one of His disciples, records the first time Jesus used the word *epiginosko*. With your lexicon open, note the two instances in verses 16 and 20 where Jesus used the word *epiginosko*.

Let's read verses 15-16 together.

> *"Beware of the false prophets, who come to you in sheep's clothing but inwardly are ravenous wolves. You will know them by their fruits. Grapes are not gathered from thornbushes, nor figs from thistles, are they?"*
> Matthew 7:15-16

What does "know" mean in Greek in verse 16? _____

_____

Continue to mine through verses 17-20.

> *"So, every good tree bears good fruit, but the bad tree bears bad fruit. A good tree cannot produce bad fruit, nor can a bad tree produce good fruit. Every tree that does not bear good fruit is cut down and thrown into the fire. So then, you will know them by their fruits."*

Once again, what does "know" mean in Greek in verse 20? _____

_____

Epiginosko holds a unique place in context when it is used in the New Testament, especially by Jesus. *Epiginosko*: to know through direct relationship. I recognize this seems like a long definition, but if you are anything like me, you might wonder why Jesus chose this form of "know" when teaching about false prophets in Matthew 7. *Epiginosko* sounds so wonderful, almost like knowing on a higher level. But I can assure you that is not the case here. However, Jesus' use of this word was intentional–*very* intentional.

Jesus issued a warning about false prophets. In the Bible, a prophet refers to anyone who is God's mouthpiece. A prophet's words carry weight and direction as they relate to the dealings of God, specifically God's plans. The Bible records those who loved God listened to prophets because they wanted to hear from God. There was a measure of trust for anyone who claimed to be a prophet of God.

With that understanding, Jesus explicitly warned the listening crowd about false prophets. Twice He used the word *epiginosko*: to know exactly through a direct relationship. Jesus provides them a way to *epiginosko* a false prophet. Basically, a false prophet bears bad fruit.

Why did Jesus use the word "*epiginosko*" in this context? To bear fruit takes time, in fact, many seasons. Fruit doesn't just show up. It is growing moment by moment until the fruit is displayed. God's prophet–His mouthpiece–is proven by his fruit. Is he leading people to look to God or, by using bits of truth, leading people to himself? A false prophet will ultimately use his self-appointed title for his own personal gain. His own personal gain equals bad fruit.

But here, I believe, is the wisdom of using the word *epiginosko*. In places of leadership, there have been men and women who have loved God but have sinned. They made poor choices. It's that simple. I do not believe Jesus is referring to them. They are sinners, as we all are, and need to repent. Here, I believe Jesus is highlighting those who, from the start, use a prophetic platform for their own personal edification and agenda. It might not be evident initially, just like young blooms on a tree, but with time–knowing exactly through direct relationship–a plethora of bad fruit is evident.

We know the law of Moses directly states we are not to bear false witness. Of course, Jesus knew that. To call someone a false prophet because of one sin or wrong choice would not have been appropriate. Call it sin, yes, but not necessarily a false prophet. Jesus intentionally used *epiginosko* to teach them to observe someone over a period of time, to know first-hand through a relationship. If the long-term fruit is bad, understand who you are dealing with–a wolf in sheep's clothing.

Continue reading Matthew 7:21-23.
Jesus said, *"Not everyone who says to me, 'Lord, Lord,' will enter the kingdom of heaven, but he who does the will of my Father who is in heaven. Many will say to Me on that day, 'Lord, Lord, did we not prophesy*

*in Your name, and in Your name cast out demons, and in Your name perform many miracles?' And then will I declare to them, '**I never knew you**; depart from me, you who practice lawlessness.'"*

"I never *knew* you." In this instance, Jesus used the word *ginosko*, to know through personal experience. In contrast to *epiginosko*, which alludes to long-term knowing, *ginosko* can be a one-time occurrence. For us, the moment we believed or put our faith in Jesus, we entered into *ginosko*. However, "I never knew you" clearly states there has never been a personal relationship with Him.

While *ginosko* and *epiginosko* are similar, Jesus clarified the difference with His word choice, didn't he? Mining, as we have been doing, allows us to see the intent behind the words of Christ.

So, how does this passage impact our lives today? How does the caution Jesus gave His followers over two thousand years ago affect us? Perhaps you can, looking back, identify a charismatic church leader in your past who ultimately led to division, destruction, and hurt within your church or place of worship, maybe even in your own family. Jesus teaches us what He thinks of those types of leaders. He does not identify with them. It's my belief we should approach these people with the same mindset. I am so grateful for our True Shepherd, Jesus Christ, who isn't afraid to call a wolf by its name.

Something to consider:

Perhaps you have been personally familiar with this type of "wolf." To what level was your trust violated? What have you needed to do to remove yourself from their leadership and their influence in your life? Has there been a family member, an authority, who used many of Jesus' words but did not have the love of Christ in his life?

_____

_____

Pray with me:
Lord, I am aware of this person in my past who said he/she was a believer, a leader, and a person who influenced my spiritual life, but the fruit of his life indicated otherwise. I was persuaded by his words, mannerisms, and compelling message, but I see now that he was not of You. Lord, release me from any word or action that this "wolf" imparted to me that did not align with Your Word. By the power of Your Holy Spirit, break any emotional or spiritual tie I have with them. Thank you for your loving protection.
In Jesus' Name, Amen.

WHEN YOUR HEART CRIES

Day 12

*"At that time Jeus said, 'I praise You, Father, Lord of heaven and earth,
that You have hidden these things from the wise and intelligent and have
revealed them to infants.
Yes, Father, for this was well pleasing in Your sight.'*

*'All things have been handed over to Me by My Father;
and no one **knows** the Son except the Father;
Nor does anyone **know** the Father except the Son,
and anyone to whom the Son wills to reveal Him.
Come to me, all who are weary and heavy-laden
and I will give you rest. Take My yoke upon you and learn from Me,
for I am gentle and humble in heart, and you will find rest for your souls.'
For my yoke is easy and My burden is light.'"*
Matthew 11:25-30

WHEN YOUR HEART CRIES

Day 12
Because I Know Him

I live in the skydiving capital of the world. Open parachutes floating through the sky are a regular visual from our DeLand home. Recently, my husband, a real estate broker, had a conversation with one of the parachute greats, Paul. He runs a parachute business and is an avid jumper himself. One day, as my husband discussed the whole process of folding and packing the parachutes, he remarked how stressful it must be. Making a mistake could be catastrophic. Paul told him that everyone packs their own chute except for him. Surprised, my husband asked who prepared and folded his parachute. Paul quietly turned to another man in the room and said, "This man packs mine." My husband inquired as to why. Paul looked him squarely in the eyes and said, "Because I *know* him. We've been partners for years, and I *know* him."

"I know him." That one statement speaks volumes in this instance, doesn't it?

That, my friends, is *epiginosko*, to know accurately through a direct relationship.

Yesterday, we saw how *epiginosko* was used with a somewhat negative connotation. Today, let's mine Matthew 11:25-30 and see how *epiginosko* is used. With your Bible and phone, look for "know" in these six verses, making notes in your Bible.

Let's take a closer look together. I noticed these three things in particular.

First, Jesus begins this portion of the passage by speaking in the first person to His Father. Matthew records this intimate moment of Jesus loving on His Father, declaring for all of those listening that He was Lord of heaven and earth.

Next, Jesus shifts his attention to those around Him and states, *"All things have been handed over to Me by my Father, and no one knows (epiginosko) the Son except the Father, nor does anyone know (epiginosko) the Father except the Son and anyone to whom the Son wills to reveal Him"* (Matthew 11:27).

Inserting our definition for *epiginosko*, it would read like this: *"No one knows accurately through direct relationship the Son except the Father, and no one knows accurately through direct relationship the Father except the Son, and anyone to whom the Son chooses to reveal Him."*

While the meaning of *epiginosko* might be cumbersome to read, it conveys such impact in context. If you are a parent, you know *epiginosko*, the relationship you have with your child, especially when they are young and under your authority. No one knows your child better than you, and no one knows you better than the child who is in a daily relationship with you.

Just like the man who packed his friend's parachute, *epiginosko* implies a trust relationship that develops over time (or, on the contrary, like yesterday's lesson, a lack of trust in the relationship). It is clear Jesus revels in His relationship with the Father. What a tender moment captured by Matthew—a snapshot to memorialize as we seek to imitate Christ in our own lives.

Ironically, the book of Luke conveys the same moment. Use your Lexicon to do a quick search for Luke 10:22.

What derivative of "know" did Luke use in retelling these very same events? _____

Why do you think Matthew used the word *epiginosko*, and Luke used *ginosko*?

We don't know for certain, but it is interesting to note that Matthew was present when Jesus made His statement, while Luke only conveyed what he heard from those who were with Jesus. Other than that, we certainly can agree this glimpse into the relationship between the Father and His Son exudes trust and respect.

We have no purer example of *epiginosko*, the ability to know accurately or with certainty through a direct relationship, than Jesus and His Father.

Secondly, Matthew 11:25 alleges that it is the Father who reveals. Yet, in verse 27, Jesus states, *". . . and anyone to whom the Son chooses to reveal Him (Father)."* That, my friends, includes you and me, *"to whom the Son chooses to reveal."* I marvel that in one breath, Jesus speaks so intimately about His relationship with God the Father, and in the next breath, He includes us. Let that sink in for a minute.

What a great love He has for His Father and His Father for Him, and yet, as believers, we are embraced and folded into this relationship. The Son invites us to *epiginosko*, His Father, to know Him accurately through a direct relationship.

That invitation is extended in Matthew 11:28-30:

> *"Come to me, all who are weary and are heavy laden, and I will give you rest. Take my yoke upon you, and learn from Me, for I am gentle and humble in heart, and you will find rest for your souls. For My yoke is easy, and My burden is light."*

"Come to me, all who labor and are heavy laden . . ." Jesus qualified who can come into relationship with His Father. Those words, labor and heavy laden, include every human suffering, sorrow, and weight. I don't know of a single one of us who doesn't, at some time, fall into that category. Yet Jesus extends hope with these words, "Come to Me."

Then He continues, *"Take my yoke upon you, and learn from Me . . ."* This is the glorious exchange. Through *epiginosko*, knowing accurately through a direct relationship, we give Him our burdens–our yoke, time after time–in exchange for His! And this is the most amazing part: He freely takes it! There isn't a time limit. He doesn't tell us to get our act together first or need anything of us. His offer doesn't require our goodness for Him to be good. His words are simply: come, take.

What do we gain? Rest. For *"you will find rest for your souls."*

If you still have your lexicon open to Matthew 11:29, you will find the Greek word for "soul." It is *psuché*, your own personality, personhood. It is you and me as unique individuals. Jesus was speaking to those who had been oppressed by the Pharisees and scribes, weighted down by their rules and requirements, but His invitation is just as valid for us today.

Come to Me.
Take from Me.
Rest in Me.

And friends, here is what I have found: the more I come, take, and rest, the more He proves His faithfulness. This is *epiginosko*, isn't it? I can know accurately through a direct relationship, which has been proven over time. And because of Jesus and His invitation to know the Father, I can keep knowing. That knowing only grows.

Consider these words from the great hymn of our faith.

"Great is Thy faithfulness, O God my Father,
There is no shadow of turning with Thee,
Thou changest not, Thy compassions, they fail not,
As Thou has been and forever will be."[2]

Something to consider:

What holds you back from coming, taking, and resting in Him? Do you feel like you have tried this before, yet circumstances haven't changed? What keeps you from epiginosko with the Father?

WHEN YOUR HEART CRIES

_____

_____

_____

Let's quiet our hearts together in prayer:
Lord, thank You for Your invitation to come to You, take from You, and rest in You. Today, I confess I have sometimes wanted things to change and circumstances to be resolved more than I have wanted You. I have measured Your love for me on my past experiences. Forgive me, Lord, when I have walked around with my yoke and thought I could handle it on my own. Help me to daily give it to You and thank You for Your willingness to take it. I desire to know (epiginosko) You more.
In Jesus' Name, Amen.

WHEN YOUR HEART CRIES

Day 13

"And behold, two of them were going that very day to a village named Emmaus, which was about seven miles from Jerusalem, And they were talking with each other about all these things which had taken place.
*While they were talking and discussing, Jesus Himself approached and began traveling with them. But their eyes were prevented from **recognizing** Him. And He said to them, 'What are these words that you are exchanging with one another as you are walking?' And they stood still, looking sad.*
One of them named Cleopas, answered and said to Him, 'Are You the only one visiting Jerusalem and unaware of the things which have happened here in these days?' And He said to them, 'What things?'
And they said to Him, 'The things about Jesus the Nazarene, who was a prophet mighty in deed and word in the sight of God and all the people, and how the chief priests and our rulers delivered Him to the sentence of death, and crucified Him. But we were hoping that it was He who was going to redeem Israel. Indeed, besides all of this, it is the third day since these things happened. But also some women among us amazed us. When they were at the tomb early in the morning, and did not find His body, they came, saying that they had also seen a vision of angels who said that He was alive. Some of those who were with us went to the tomb and found it just exactly as the women also had said; but Him they did not see.'

And He said to them, 'O foolish men and slow of heart to believe in all that the prophets have spoken! Was it not necessary for the Christ to suffer these things and to enter into His glory?' Then beginning with Moses and with all the prophets, He explained to them the things concerning Himself in all the Scriptures. And they approached the village where they were going, and He acted as though He were going farther. But they urged Him, saying, 'Stay with us, for it is getting toward evening, and the day is now nearly over.' So He went in to stay with them.

*When He had reclined (at the table) with them, He took the bread and blessed it, and breaking it, He began giving it to them. Then their eyes were opened and they **recognized** Him; and He vanished from their sight.*
They said to one another, 'Were not our hearts burning within us while He was speaking to us on the road, while He was explaining the Scriptures to us?'
And they got up that very hour and returned to Jerusalem, and found gathered together the eleven and those who were with them, saying,
'The Lord has really risen and has appeared to Simon.'
*They began to relate their experiences on the road and how He was **recognized** by them in the breaking of the bread."*
Luke 24:13-35

WHEN YOUR HEART CRIES

Day 13
The Seven Mile Walk that Changed Everything

Have you ever lost someone close to you? Grief can become the overriding condition, can't it? This is where we find a couple of men, Cleopas, and an unnamed companion in Luke 24:13-35.

As we mine these verses, let's remember, we skim read with the purpose of finding the word "know" or another English word that translates "know" in Greek: recognize, realize, or understand. Then, we'll go back and dive deeper into the context.

What derivative of the word "know" did you find in Luke 24:16? _____
What about verse 31? _____
And verse 35? _____

Now, let's look closer at the passage. It begins on the first day of the week, three days after Jesus was crucified. For the believers of Jesus, hearts were heavy, and questions swirling as conflicting stories began to emerge. First, the women who followed Jesus were frightened at His tomb by two men declaring it was empty and that He had risen. Then, both John and Peter discovered an empty tomb and no men around as reported, yet they left to share their findings with *". . . the eleven and to all the rest"* (Luke 24:9). The overriding question is, "Where was Jesus?"

On that very same day, scripture records two men, Cleopas, and his companion, leaving Jerusalem and traveling the seven-mile hike to Emmaus. Grief and disbelief framed their conversation, which centered around all that had occurred. At that moment, *". . . Jesus himself drew near and went with them"* (Luke 24:15).

Yet *". . . their eyes were kept from recognizing him"* (Luke 24:16). "Recognize" (*epiginosko*) to know accurately through a direct relationship. The use of this word indicates they previously had a direct relationship with Jesus. They knew Him. They had spent time with Him. It is believed Cleopas and his friend were two of the seventy disciples Jesus sent out to minister earlier in Luke 10. Scripture tells us that in Jesus' name, they healed the sick and cast out demons. They experienced tremendous success in their short ministry. Yet, here was Jesus with them, in the flesh, and they did not *recognize* Him.

Did God intervene and blur their vision? Did God intentionally adjust what they saw? Most theologians believe it was not an act of God that kept them from recognizing Jesus. Simply, it was where they placed their eyes. Their sight was no longer on Jesus or remembering all He had promised. Their mental gaze had shifted to the confusing reports, and in grief, they lowered their eyes, *". . . looking sad"* (Luke 24:17).

While they narrated their record of events in verses Luke 24:18-24, it is verse 21 that tells the real story.

"But we had hoped . . ." That is past tense. These men lost hope because they lost focus on Jesus. Despite all of the time He had invested in them, they lost hope because they shifted their gaze to a crucified Jesus and an empty tomb. Now, they were walking away.

For them, Jesus' death was like a period at the end of a sentence. Finished. The end. Hopeless.
Or was it?

Read how Jesus responds to them in verse 25. In essence, He rebuked them. *". . . O foolish ones, and slow of heart to believe all the prophets have spoken!"* (Luke 24:25).

They saw themselves as hopeless; Jesus saw them as slow of heart. We learned the Greek for "heart" on Day 5. Remember? It means *kardia*: our mind, will, and emotions. Jesus was not rebuking them for grieving and being sad. He corrected them because they allowed their minds and emotions to overshadow everything He taught them. They had already forgotten what mighty miracles they performed in His name. They had forgotten His promises.

When sorrow hits us, it is perfectly appropriate to grieve, but we cannot allow circumstances and bad reports to overrule the Word of God. When we do, we will most assuredly lose hope.

Then, Jesus does what Jesus does. He shifts their thinking to what is true. *"And beginning with Moses and with all the Prophets, He explained to them the things concerning Himself in all Scriptures"* (Luke 24:27).

Can you imagine listening to that account?

The seven-mile walk ended with an invitation for Jesus to stay with the men for the evening. Then the moment came, *". . . he (Jesus) took the bread and blessed and broke it and began giving it to them. Then their eyes were opened, and they recognized (epiginosko) Him"* (Luke 24:30-31).

"They recognized Him." It took seven miles, about two hours of walking, and the patient Teacher connecting centuries of prophecy for these two men to "know accurately through direct relationship" that their Savior was indeed alive!

As a matter of fact, after they realized they had been with Jesus, they turned right back around and walked those same seven miles returning to Jerusalem (maybe even ran a bit!). Rejoicing, they came back to the upper room with this report, *"He was recognized (ginosko, through personal experience) by them in the breaking of the bread"* (Luke 24:35).

No, Christ's death was not a period; it was not the end of the story.

It was part of the fulfillment of prophecy and, because of the resurrection, the beginning of a life that is abundant and free for all those who believe in Jesus. It is a life filled with hope regardless of our circumstances because He alone is our Hope (1 Timothy 1:1).

Something to consider:

Even as a Christian, there have been times when I have lost hope because I have fixed my eyes on challenging circumstances. I am unable to see any way to move forward or anything positive about the situation. Then He calls, and I have to adjust my gaze. What holds your focus today? What is Jesus speaking to your heart?

_____

_____

_____

"Why are you in despair, O my soul? And why are you disturbed within me? Hope in God, for I shall again praise Him, the help of my countenance and my God."
Psalm 43:5

Pray with me:
Lord, it is always easier to see how others, like these men, lose their focus on You when grief sets in. However, I know there have been times when I, too, have lost heart during challenging circumstances. Thank You for Your Spirit, who lives within me, constantly guiding me into all truth. Thank You that You have never left me or forsaken me.
In Jesus' Name, Amen.

Day 14

*"If I speak in the tongues of men and of angels, but do not have love, I have become a noisy gong or a clanging cymbal. If I have the gift of prophecy, and **know** all mysteries and all **knowledge** and if I have all faith, so as to remove mountains, but do not have love, I am nothing. If I give all my possessions to feed the poor, and if I surrender my body to be burned, but have not love, it profits me nothing.*

Love is patient, love is kind and is not jealous, love does not brag and is not arrogant, does not act unbecomingly; It does not seek its own, is not provoked, does not take into account a wrong suffered, does not rejoice in unrighteousness, but rejoices with the truth; Love bears all things, believes all things, hopes all things, endures all things.

*"Love never fails; but if there are gifts of prophecy, they will be done away; if there are tongues, they will cease; if there is **knowledge**, it will be done away. For we **know** in part and we prophesy in part, but when the perfect comes, the partial will be done away. When I was a child, I used to speak like a child, think like a child, reason like a child; when I became a man, I did away with childish things.*

*For now we see in a mirror dimly, but then face to face, now I **know** in part; but then I will **know** fully, just as I also have **been fully known**. So now faith, hope, and love abide, these three; but the greatest of these is love."*
1 Corinthians 13:1-13

WHEN YOUR HEART CRIES

Day 14
To Be an Honest Player

A horn player exited the stage after a triumphant display of orchestral brilliance. As a student, John felt quite impressed with his performance. He had never played so well and was prepared to hear the praises of his professor. However, when his teacher met up with him, his wise assessment left a lasting impression. "John, you played your heart out today. But you got lucky. We both know that you haven't practiced enough to play that well. If you want to succeed, you need to become an honest player."

I can relate to that, can't you? Many times in my daily life, I give myself a little pat on the back for doing something out of the ordinary: taking a meal to someone, serving outside the church, or extending a kindness when not warranted. But I know in my heart I'm not always an honest player. I'm not consistently yielding my life to Christ so He might minister through me as He wills.

Paul addressed something similar with the church in Corinth. The Christians there were boldly speaking in tongues, prophesying, and performing miracles within the body. All of that was good, yet Paul makes a statement that leaves the same kind of lasting impression.

He says, *". . . earnestly desire the greater gifts. And I show you a still more excellent way."* (1 Corinthians 12:31).

Paul was ready to prove to these former Gentiles, now Christ followers, how to be honest players in "a more excellent way." And quite honestly, isn't that our greatest desire?

Let's follow Paul while we continue to mine the word "know." I think you are going to be surprised by what we find. I know I was.

Turn in your Bible and open your phone to 1 Corinthians 13:1 in your Lexicon, mining this short chapter. You'll recognize this passage as one frequently recited in weddings, the "love chapter." However, these verses are sandwiched between two chapters that focus on the use of spiritual gifts within the church. Why would Paul interrupt his flow of teaching on how the body of Christ should conduct itself by inserting a seemingly different lesson?

I believe Paul wanted the Corinthians to be honest players. Let's look at what that means.

As we read the chapter, the word "know" (or a form of the word) is used seven times.

"If I speak in the tongues of men and of angels, but do not have love, I have become a noisy gong or a clanging cymbal. If I have the gift of prophecy, and know (oida, because I have seen or perceived) all mysteries and all knowledge (gnosis, knowledge gained through personal experience) and if I have all faith, so as to remove mountains, but do not have love, I am nothing. If I give all my possessions to feed the poor, and if I surrender my body to be burned, but have not love, it profits me nothing" (1 Corinthians 13:1-3).

Paul uses the word "know" to frame his argument. The church members can speak in tongues, openly prophesy, and declare tremendous faith, but if there isn't love–the love of Christ–they aren't honest players. They might do the right things, but they may not be honest players.

Paul continues by stating what an honest player would look like: *"Love is patient, love is kind and is not jealous, love does not brag and is not arrogant, does not act unbecomingly; It does not seek its own, is not provoked, does not take into account a wrong suffered, does not rejoice in unrighteousness, but rejoices with the truth; Love bears all things, believes all things, hopes all things, endures all things"* (1 Corinthians 13:4-7).

While there's not a derivative of "know" in these verses for us to mine, it's important to note that Paul shares something fundamental. He is preparing to state his case in the next few verses. Watch for the shift in his wording.

*"Love never fails; but if there are gifts of prophecy, they will be done away; if there are tongues, they will cease; if there is knowledge (**gnosis**, knowledge gained through personal experience), it will be done away. For we know (**ginosko**, through personal experience) in part and we prophesy in part, but when the perfect comes, the partial will be done away. When I was a child, I used to speak like a child, think like a child, reason like a child; when I became a man, I did away with childish things.*

*For now we see in a mirror dimly, but then face to face, **now I know** (ginosko, through personal experience) in part; but **then I will know** (epiginosko, to know accurately through direct relationship) fully, just as I also **have been fully known** (epiginosko, to know accurately through direct relationship). So now faith, hope, and love abide, these three; but the greatest of these is love."*
1 Corinthians 13:8-13

Paul has moved from *ginosko* to *epiginosko*. Now, we *ginosko* in part, but then we will *epiginosko*, as we have already been *epiginoskoed*!

It is eternity that moves us from *ginosko*, knowing in part, to *epiginosko*, to know fully. It is not the gifts used in the body of Christ that makes the difference. It is the virtues of faith, hope, and love, the greatest being love.

Gifts were given to glorify God and edify the body. But if we want to be used by Him and become truly fruitful, we must recognize it is His love in us making the difference. He has chosen us to be the instruments of love to others. Love brings lasting change and the greatest impact. Like extensive practice for the horn player, love is the one thing that makes us an honest player. Love sets us apart.

Why? Because there will be a time when prophecy and speaking in unknown tongues will cease and when healing will no longer be needed. But it is the virtues of faith, hope, and love that transcend eternity. And it is love, Paul argues, that is the greatest difference maker in our lives. Love never fails. It is through ministering in love that we become honest players.

God pours out His love to us so that we might pour out His love to others. Gifts have their rightful place within the body, but without love, they are not fruitful for the kingdom of God.

Oh, we see in a mirror dimly, but there will be a day when you and I get to know, *epiginosko*, as we have already known, *epiginosko*. He looks at me, a sinner, yet knows, *epiginosko*, me. And He loves me, and He loves you. What a motivation to extend that same love to others.

Something to consider:

To be an honest player as a Christian can look wonderful on paper, can't it? But what about those difficult relationships? I believe you, like me, want to put forth the love of Christ whenever we are called to. You want to be an honest player. I, too, have those same relationship challenges, but this is what I have found. I have learned to focus on the epiginosko, my relationship with Christ. I remind myself He knows me fully through direct relationship. We have a trust relationship that's been proven. There is not a difficult earthly relationship that can destroy or minimize my relationship with Christ. When I focus on Him and how He knows me and loves me, then I am better equipped to hear from Him in how to love others, even in difficult relationships. That is my desire, and I'm sure it is yours as well, to become an honest player. What does this lesson on being an honest player mean for you?

Pray with me:
Lord, more than anything, it is my desire to know You more each day, so I can walk with confidence regardless of the circumstances. I want to be an honest player, not just look like one. I want to put the time into our relationship so that my life reflects what is true and honest. Fill my heart with Your love, Lord, so I might be an extension of You.
In Jesus' Name, Amen.

WHEN YOUR HEART CRIES

WHEN YOUR HEART CRIES

Day 15

(Paul writes) "Blessed be the God and Father of our Lord Jesus Christ, the Father of mercies and the God of all comfort, who comforts us in all our affliction so that we will be able to comfort those who are in any affliction with the comfort with which we ourselves are comforted by God.

*For just as the sufferings of Christ are ours in abundance, so also our comfort is abundant through Christ. But if we are afflicted, it is for your comfort and salvation; or if we are comforted, it is for your comfort, which is effective in the patient enduring of the same sufferings which we also suffer; And our hope for you is firmly grounded, **knowing** that as you are sharers of our sufferings, so also you are sharers of our comfort.*

For we do not want you to be unaware, brethren, of our affliction which came to us in Asia, that we were burdened excessively beyond our strength, so that we despaired even of life; indeed we had the sentence of death within ourselves so that we would not trust in ourselves, but in God who raises the dead; who delivered us from so great a peril of death, and will deliver us, He on whom we have our hope, And He will yet deliver us, you also joining in helping us through your prayers, so that thanks may be given by many persons on our behalf for the favor bestowed on us through the prayers of many.

For our proud confidence is this: the testimony of our conscience, that in holiness and godly sincerity, not in fleshly wisdom but in the grace of God, we have conducted ourselves in the world, and especially toward you.

*For we write nothing else to you than what you read and **understand**, and I hope you will **understand** until the end; just as you also partially did **understand** us, that we are your reason to be proud as you also are ours in the day of our Lord Jesus. In this confidence I intended at first to come to you, so that you might twice receive a blessing; That is to pass your way into Macedonia, and again from Macedonia to come to you, and by you to be helped on my journey to Judea. Therefore, I was not vacillating when I intended to do this, was I? Or what I purpose, do I purpose according to the flesh, so that with me there will be yes, yes and no, no at the same time? But as God is faithful our word to you is not yes and no. For the Son of God, Christ Jesus, who was preached among you by us- by me and Silvanus and Timothy- was not yes and no, but is Yes in Him. For as many as are the promises of God, in Him they are yes; therefore also through Him is our Amen to the glory of God through us. Now He who establishes us with you in Christ and anointed us is God, who also sealed us and gave us the Spirit in our hearts as a pledge."*

2 Corinthians 1:3-22

WHEN YOUR HEART CRIES

Day 15
The Bridge Builder

The apostle Paul was a bridge builder. No, not by trade. Paul was a bridge builder by calling. Never is this more evident than in 2 Corinthians 1:3-22.

Let's take a minute to mine these verses. Once again, we are mining for the word "know" or a derivative of the word frequently used by Paul, "understand." Also, as you skim read, please note and underline each time Paul uses the words "we" and "us."

Now, let's mine 2 Corinthians 1:3-22.

You might have lost count, but Paul used the words "we" and "us" over two dozen times just in this passage.

The words "we' and "us" are bridge-building words, aren't they? They are words we use to include, not set apart. Paul was writing to the church of Corinth yet again, this time refuting claims from a small minority who still questioned his authority and calling. Many had repented of this thinking, which was certainly cause for rejoicing. However, a small group of Judaizers remained. Paul could have verbally taken them to task by attacking them personally or calling them out by name. But Paul knew his role. He was called to be a bridge builder, a unifier, for the sake of the gospel of Jesus Christ. Therefore, he used the inclusive words "we" and "us" to state his case. Even his initial greeting united himself with them, *"Grace to you and peace from God **our** Father and the Lord Jesus Christ"* (2 Corinthians 1:2).

Now, using this context as our setting, let's look at the word "know" and see how Paul used it within this passage.

The first instance of "know" is in 2 Corinthians 1:6-7, where Paul addresses the church at Corinth.

"If we are afflicted, it is for your comfort and salvation; or if we are comforted, it is for your comfort, which is effective in the patient enduring of the same sufferings which we also suffer. And our hope for you is firmly grounded, **knowing** *(oida, having seen it or perceived it) that as you are sharers in our sufferings, so also you are sharers of our comfort"* (2 Corinthians 1:6-7).

A common belief in the early church was that if someone suffered in any way, God must be punishing them. This erroneous thinking was a verdict of sorts: suffering equated to being out of right standing with God. Paul, being a bridge builder, uses his own life story to contradict that belief. In fact, he employs it as an opportunity to declare the deliverance of God in his life, not the punishment of God.

". . . knowing that as you are sharers of our sufferings, so also you are sharers of our comfort" (2 Corinthians 1:7).

Our sufferings, our comfort–a bridge builder's words.

Take a moment to look at how Paul addresses the Corinthian believers in verses 3-7 using "we" and "us" phrases:
- Who comforts us
- we may be able to comfort
- we ourselves are comforted by God
- we share abundantly in Christ's sufferings
- through Christ, we share abundantly
- we are afflicted
- we are comforted
- we suffer, but our hope in You is unshaken

When I experienced a difficult season in my life, Paul's words provided me with so much hope, direction, and consolation.

Now, I challenge you. Skim through 2 Corinthians 1:8-11 and briefly write out the "we" and "us" statements below as we did above. (I've only listed eight instances, but there are more.)

- _____
- _____
- _____
- _____
- _____
- _____
- _____
- _____

Do you see Paul's pattern?

With every opportunity, he chose to unify. His words were purposeful.

He wanted to bring together Christians, Jews, and Gentiles, those who were previously led astray by false teachers, and those who still needed to repent. At every turn, he included himself as part of them. That is why, as we read 2 Corinthians 1:13-14, we glean even more from mining Paul's carefully chosen words.

*"For we write nothing else to you than what you read and understand (**epiginosko**, know exactly through direct relationship) and I hope you will understand (**epiginosko**, know exactly through direct relationship) until the end; just as you also partially did understand (**epiginosko**, know exactly through direct relationship) us–that we are your reason to be proud as you also are ours in the day of our Lord Jesus"* (2 Corinthians 1:13-14).

Why would Paul use *epiginosko* three times in this passage? _____

What have we learned about *epiginosko*? _____
_____

Paul, by using *epiginosko*, implies a relationship that is ongoing and certain, a relationship with history.

What they know and what they will know will ultimately come through a relationship. It implies that no matter what, he wasn't walking away. Despite the difficulties, and there had been a few, he was there for the long haul.

Let's close with a look at Paul's words in verses 2 Corinthians 1:21-22.

"Now He who establishes us with you in Christ, and anointed us in God, who also sealed us and gave us the Spirit in our hearts as a pledge" (2 Corinthians 1:21-22).

Did you catch how many times Paul used that sweet word again, "us"? Together, we have *epiginosko* because of our personal relationship with Christ. He establishes us, anoints us, and seals us with His Spirit.

Yes, Jesus Christ is the ultimate Bridge Builder.

God looked at the vast chasm that separated us as sinners and Himself and sent His Son, Jesus, to bridge that gap so we might have the opportunity to know Him. Not just *oida*, but *ginosko* and *epiginosko*. For those of us who have received Christ, including the church of Corinth, He became our spiritual bridge to the Father, His Spirit as a guarantee.

Something to consider:

When hard times have been a part of my journey, I have wanted answers and direction. My prayer sounded something like this: "Just tell me what to do, Lord, and I'll do it."

What I didn't realize at the time was in those hard, lonely times, the Lord desired for me to know Him more, not just give me marching orders. He wanted me to learn to hear His voice and give me an opportunity to respond. He was building *epiginosko* in our relationship. There were times I stumbled, other times I ran, and still other times I soared. He is equipping you, too, for plans yet to be revealed. I believe that with all my heart. Could it be we are called to be bridge builders as well?

Please take a moment and write down what you hear the Lord speaking to you.
_____
_____
_____

Pray with me:
Lord, may I be more like Paul. Lead me as I commit to being a bridge builder to those I am in relationship with. May my life be a testimony of love for others.
In Jesus' Name, Amen.

Tomorrow, we turn the page. I can't wait to show you what we will be studying!

WHEN YOUR HEART CRIES

Outliers

WHEN YOUR HEART CRIES

Day 16

*"Now concerning things sacrificed to idols, we **know** that we all have **Knowledge**. **Knowledge** makes arrogant, but love edifies."*
1 Corinthians 8:1

*"Woe to you lawyers: For you have taken away the key of **knowledge**; you yourselves did not enter, and you hindered those who were entering."*
Luke 11:52

*"More than that, I count all things to be loss in view of the surpassing value of **knowing** Christ Jesus my Lord, for whom I have suffered the loss of all things, and count
them but rubbish so that I may gain Christ."*
Philippians 3:8

WHEN YOUR HEART CRIES

Day 16
The Real Thing

The chemical equation for plain white sugar is $C_{12}H_{22}O_{11}$. I'm not a chemist, but I certainly know how sweet sugar is! I find it interesting that every couple of years, a new and better sweetener is introduced and marketed as the next greatest sugar substitute. And while they may be sweet, not one can claim to be authentic sugar–the real thing.

For the last fifteen days, you have mined the New Testament for the word "know." Together, we have learned the difference between the verbs *oida*, *ginosko*, and *epiginosko*. But today, we are going to discuss an outlier. It is *gnosis*, a noun with the root of *ginosko*, but just like sugar, you'll see how the world has created a knockoff–a counterfeit.

First, let's look at the authentic *gnosis*. *Gnosis* is a noun which means "the knowledge gained from personal experience." It is used twenty-nine times in the New Testament. *Gnosis* has a broad interpretation completely based on the circumstances in which it's used.

For instance, in 1 Corinthians 8:1, Paul states, *". . . we know (oida) that 'all of us possess knowledge (gnosis).' This 'knowledge' (gnosis) puffs up, but love builds up."* You can add the definition of gnosis as you re-read it, "the knowledge gained from personal experience."

Then we have the account of Jesus' rebuke in Luke 11:52, *"Woe to you lawyers! For you have taken away the key of knowledge (gnosis). You did not enter yourselves (into the Kingdom), and you hindered those who were entering."* Once again, you can add the definition of gnosis as you reread this verse.

And yet another example of gnosis in Philippians 3:8, *"Indeed, I count everything as loss because of the surpassing worth of knowing (gnosis) Christ Jesus my Lord."*

Gnosis, a noun meaning "the knowledge gained from personal experience." It can be quite profound, right?

But the truth about *gnosis* is that this knowledge is only as valid as the object in which we place it. If our knowledge is in Jesus Christ, we can stand on solid ground. Unfortunately, about the second century AD, a counterfeit "knowledge" made its way onto the scene. This counterfeit knowledge was the very basis for Gnosticism.

In short, Gnosticism became the knockoff and cloaked itself in the supernatural. This "religion" was a non-Christian group that believed they had special esoteric knowledge, *gnosis*. They believed our physical bodies, those God declared good in Genesis, were defiled. Their beliefs equated Yahweh of the Old Testament to an evil god who erroneously created all physical matter, including the earth. Gnosticism encouraged the defilement of the human body to achieve a higher spiritual state, a higher *gnosis*. They denied Jesus, the resurrected body of Christ, and His deity.

While this sounds somewhat outlandish to us as Christians, Gnosticism still has its tentacles in our world today. Think of the "religions" proclaiming power but have no foundation in the gospel of Jesus Christ. There is a prevalent religion that teaches if we work to fix ourselves, we can be more like God. Their position is that we can attain a higher knowledge and walk on a higher plain. In addition, there is New Age spiritual teaching, witchcraft, and satanic worship, now accepted as religious freedom. There is pantheism—worship of rocks, stones, stars, and planets. Sexual immorality of any kind is justified because of sincerely seeking a higher knowledge. These types of *gnosis* have no absolutes. Gnosticism identifies itself as "very spiritual" but lacks a Biblical foundation.

Remember what we stated earlier. Our knowledge, *gnosis*, is only as valid as the object in which we place it. And just like the analogy of real sugar and its counterfeits, there have been and will continue to be those who profess to be spiritual but have nothing to do with the real thing: the gospel of Jesus. They take a bit of truth and distort it to fit their beliefs.

God's word provides the acid test:

"Beloved, do not believe every spirit, but test the spirits to see whether they are from God, because many false prophets have gone out into the world. By this you know (ginosko) the Spirit of God: every spirit that confesses that Jesus Christ has come in the flesh is from God; and every spirit that does not confess Jesus is not from God. This is the spirit of the antichrist, which you have heard that it is coming, and now it is already in the world" (1 John 4:1-3).

I believe more than ever, we need to look through the lens of God's word to judge which knowledge is truly from Him and which is not. During hardship, we can look for help in the one-inch square of our social media page or listen to a "Christian" podcast claiming to be self-help and spiritual, but Jesus as the Redeemer is never mentioned. Does what we place our attention on pass the litmus test; does it line up with the Word? Still others of you feel called to ministry but lack the confidence to proceed. I can personally share it is the knowledge of His Word and yielding to His voice that has allowed me to meet the needs of those I have been honored to pray for and serve. There is no substitute for His Word.

This is the profound impact that mining can have on us. It further grounds us in His Word. It creates a wider chasm from the knowledge, *gnosis*, of this world and that which we know is Truth. Mining provides a greater opportunity for us to experience Him and declare His goodness to this world. Through mining scripture, we see and hear Him.

"Oh, taste and see that the Lord is good! How blessed is the man who takes refuge in Him!"
Psalm 34:8

Something to consider:

Even as I write, I'm convicted of the times I've embraced "spiritual" sayings, quick one-liners, or even a social media post. Yet, upon clearer investigation, I find the originator of these statements has no basis in Christ. I am staring head-on at a counterfeit.

How do you monitor the "knowledge" that builds the framework of your daily thoughts? How can mining deepen our ability to minister to others?

_____

_____

_____

_____

_____

Pray with me:
Lord, I believe that Your knowledge, gnosis, is absolute truth. Allow me to be grounded in Your Truth. Give me eyes to see and ears to hear what Your Spirit is saying and lead me into all truth that I may be equipped to serve others.
In Jesus' Name, Amen.

Day 17

*"No longer do I call you slaves, for the slave does not **know** what his master is doing; but I have called you friends, for all things that I have heard from My Father
I have made **known** to you."*
John 15:5

*"And I have made Your name **known** to them, and will make it **known** so that the love with which You love Me may be in them, and I in them."*
John 17:26

WHEN YOUR HEART CRIES

Day 17
To Make Known

"What He wanted to do in me was far greater than what I wanted Him to do for me. I just didn't know it."

Those words I penned on a scrap of paper emerged from yet another conversation with a woman who found herself alone through no fault of her own. Her world imploded, leaving her lost, hurt, and directionless.

I remember that feeling and reality all too well. Questions seem to outweigh answers. Hurt overrides love. Hopelessness and grief become the roommates of the heart, and you wonder if you will ever be the same. I've been there.

But I learned what He wanted to do *in me* was far greater than what I wanted Him to do *for me*. I have put my arms around literally dozens of women who have found this to be their reality. Together we have cried, talked of betrayal, and tried to sort through the collateral damage. But the greatest gift I have been able to extend is this threefold promise: you are not alone, you will make it, and even though you might not feel it, God is at work in you and for you.

As we have mined the word "know" these last few days, I want to share a second outlier with you. It is *gnorizo*, a verb meaning the "act of giving knowledge, certainty." In essence, to make clear.

When I was at my lowest, wondering how God could help me, He gave me knowledge, certainty, and clarity over time. While I was praying for a restored relationship, He was giving me what I really needed—Himself.

You may not be in the situation I described above, but my guess is you know all too well seasons of deep grief and uncertainty. Perhaps it is the loss of a child or the dream of having one. Maybe you fight financial devastation or a chronic illness. Or perhaps, you feel called to minister to women in a Bible Study or small group, and it's just not happening. I can tell you: He is there.

I believe the best way to equip for troubling times in this world is to know, *ginosko*, His Word. No matter the circumstances, when we wield His Word with confidence and certainty, it destroys the enemy and provides a hurting heart with real promise and security far greater than any personal encouragement. Through His Word, He gives us Himself. I can tell you from personal experience He will meet you right where you are. Crying in your car or weeping on the floor, you can find yourself begging for answers. But He is ready to give you what you need.

This is how I know . . .

The Bible records a unique word, *gnorizo*. It is a derivative of the word *ginosko*, to know through personal experience, and is used twenty-five times in the New Testament. *Gnorizo* is what I call a "giving word." It describes the action of giving knowledge, certainty, or clarity.

I've mined a couple of examples of *gnorizo*. I pray they bless you the way they did me.

Turn in your Bible to John 15:15. Take the time to use your Greek lexicon to mine this verse.

"No longer do I call you slaves, for the slave does not know what his master is doing; but I have called you friends, for all things that I have heard from My Father I have made known (gnorizo, give knowledge, certainty, or clarity) to you."

First, Jesus is telling His disciples (and us) that He calls them friends, not rejected or worthless, not barren or "past their prime." No, He calls us His friend. Secondly, Jesus said all He has heard from His Father, He has made known to us. Not only does Jesus call me friend, but He (*gnorizo*) makes all things known to me. He makes known all things to you as well. That is the act of *gnorizo*, giving you knowledge, certainty, and clarity even in the darkest of days. He gives us what we need when we need it.

Our second passage is John 17:26. Turn in your Bible to this verse and mine it on your phone.

"And I have made Your name known, gnorizo (give knowledge, certainty, or clarity), to them, and will make it known (gnorizo give knowledge, certainty, or clarity), so that the love with which You love Me may be in them, and I in them."

You probably recognize this verse. Jesus is praying in the Garden of Gethsemane before His arrest. He is fully aware of what is about to happen to Him, yet we are on His heart. He says, "I have made Your name known, *gnorizo*, and will make it known, *gnorizo*."

What name could that be? Scripture tells us that Jesus gave us permission to call God, Father.

In Matthew 6:9, Jesus gives us these words, *"Our Father, who is in heaven, Hallowed be Your name."* Throughout the gospels, when Jesus is teaching, He refers to God as "your Father." In essence, He was saying He had given knowledge, certainty, and clarity to us so "the love with which You (God) love Me (Jesus), may be in them (us) and I in them."

In difficult times, honestly, we may not feel loved. But this is where our faith intersects God's Word. Feelings are fleeting, but we know His name is above any other name. His Word never changes, nor does His love for us. He gives us knowledge, certainty, or clarity so we might know His love.

How great is God's love for us.

If you are in a difficult season, I pray you know He wants to do something much greater in you than what you are asking Him to do for you. He is indeed a giving Father. Stand back and watch . . . He will move on your behalf again.

Something to consider:

Think of a time, perhaps even recently, when God made Himself known to you through His Word. Maybe it was an aspect of Him that you knew about but never experienced until He spoke to you through His Word? Let me give you an example. Growing up, my father worked a lot of hours to provide for us and wasn't always available. His family meant everything to him, and he gave us way more than he had ever experienced growing up. I never questioned his love for me. However, as I got older and difficult times became part of my story, I would pray but didn't really see the Father completely available to me. My mindset was, I'll pray, and when He gets around to it, He'll answer my prayer. I was allowing my past schema of a father to dictate my belief about my Heavenly Father. It took living in His Word to reframe that belief to what is true: "I (Jesus) have made all things known to you (me) . . ." I didn't have to beg, cry, or wait. He was there all along. Through His Word and His Spirit, He made Himself known to me. It changed my perspective of the Father.

Can you think of a similar time when His Word changed your thinking and allowed you to know Him more?

_____

_____

_____

_____

Pray with me:
Father, thank You for revealing Your Word to our hearts and minds. We know Your knowledge is as valid today as it was two thousand years ago. Help us to know You so that we, too, can make You known. And bring about Your knowledge, certainty, and clarity to our lives in Your sovereign time and way.
In Jesus' Name, Amen.

WHEN YOUR HEART CRIES

Day 18

*(Paul speaking) " . . . You yourselves **know** from the first day that I set foot in Asia, how I was with you the whole time, serving the Lord with all humility and with tears and with trials which came upon me through the plots of the Jews."*
Acts 20:18-19

*" . . . I **know** that all of you among whom I went about preaching the kingdom will no longer see my face. Therefore I testify to you this day that I am innocent of the blood of all men, for I did not shrink from declaring to you the whole purpose of God."*
Acts 20:25-27

WHEN YOUR HEART CRIES

Day 18
To Build Upon

It seems like we have an app for everything these days: shopping, calorie counting, finding the best restaurant, and even Google, the app we are using to mine. They certainly can be convenient. With the touch of our fingers, we can add new knowledge to our current understanding quite effortlessly.

Adding additional knowledge can be important. But as we mine the word "know," we uncover a third outlier. It is a word that means "to build upon." This Greek word is *epistamai*. (Yes, you can use the Google app to hear the pronunciation!)

We learned on Day 11 that *"epi-"* is a prefix elevating the meaning of a base word. *"Stamai"* means to stand. Together, *epistamai* refers to "gaining knowledge or building upon prior knowledge." It appears fourteen times in the New Testament and has a similar definition as some of our other Greek words. It is, however, unique in that it appears to use a "middle voice." That means the subject both acts and is impacted by the action. While this is noteworthy, *epistamai* gains its importance for the believer in the message and impact of scripture. Let's mine one of these verses.

Turn to Acts 20:18-19 in your Bible as well as the Greek Lexicon on your phone. We find Paul speaking to the elders in Ephesus.

" . . . You yourselves know (epistamai, building upon your current knowledge), from the first day that I set foot in Asia, how I was with you

the whole time, serving the Lord with all humility and with tears and with trials which came upon me through the plots of the Jews."

Paul wasn't addressing just any group of Christians. He was speaking to the overseers–the elders.

He continues in verses 25-27, *". . . I know (oida, because I've seen it or perceived it) that all of you among whom I went about preaching the kingdom will no longer see my face. Therefore I testify to you this day that I am innocent of the blood of all men, for I did not shrink from declaring to you the whole purpose of God"* (Acts 20:25-27).

You "will no longer see my face."

Paul is passing the mantle of the gospel to them once and for all, preparing them for what lies ahead. He will not always be with them. The truth and purity of the gospel have been entrusted to them, the elders of His sheep, the Church.

The Greek word *epistamai* is completely appropriate here. These men had a long-term personal relationship and experience with Paul and the gospel, or they would not have been chosen to be elders. They had a prior understanding of Jesus. In Acts 20:25-27, Paul adds to their understanding by being direct and to the point. The price was too high to leave any misunderstanding.

The *Discovery Bible* notes this:
"*Epistamai*, building on standing knowledge, is the root of *epistemology*, 'coming to know.' *Epistemology* preeminently relates to learning based upon the written Word in conjunction with knowing the living Word, hearing God's voice, experiencing faith."[3]

Looking back, we know that Paul's impact far exceeded this church in Ephesus. His willingness to obey Christ resulted in imprisonments, beatings, shipwrecks, and being left for dead. He dealt with demonic forces in magicians and soothsayers and was the object of lies and accusations. His spiritual authority was questioned in and out of the church.

Yet today, we credit Paul with writing thirteen books in the New Testament that provide theological grounding for believers everywhere. In the thirty years after Jesus' ascension, Paul preached and established churches in many cities. As a result, the gospel of Jesus spread to Asia Minor, Greece, Macedonia, Italy, Cyprus, Judea, and Syria. He left his imprint by equipping church leadership throughout his ministry as he boldly preached about Christ and the message of salvation through grace. He challenged the most intellectual leaders, overturned bloody pagan altars, closed temple doors laden with idols, and proclaimed the gospel message of Christ to all who would listen. He sat with kings and foot soldiers alike, yet even in the face of ridicule and death, his message did not waver.

My friends, Paul's profound testimony wasn't the result of just building knowledge, *epistamai*. No, his Christian life and ministry were profound because of the relationship he had with Jesus. While a phone app can add information and knowledge, it cannot produce the power of the Holy Spirit in our lives. You see, Paul didn't place his trust in what he knew; he placed his trust in Who he knew.

Something to consider:

I wonder if Paul while facing constant persecution, had any idea of the impact he would have on building leadership and a foundation for the church. And what about us? Could God be calling us to ministry, something specifically tailored just for us? I believe the Lord is speaking to many of you right now. He is asking you, like Paul, to not just build knowledge, but to trust Him for the next steps you need to take. Please say, "yes." I'm excited and praying for you! What do you need to say "yes" to?

_____

_____

Pray with me:
Lord, I know with all my heart that You have a calling on my life. I know You might be preparing me for ministry, or I find myself embedded in ministry. Either way, I long to pursue the purposes of God in my life. I declare that my life belongs to You. Apart from You, I can do nothing. But in You, I can do all things through Christ, Who strengthens me. I desire to experience Your hand in my life each day so I, like Paul, can build my life on You and Your Word.
In Jesus' Name, Amen.

Tomorrow is our final day of "outliers." I have saved the best for last!

Day 19

*"And they prayed and said, 'You, Lord, who **know** the hearts of all, show which one of these two you have chosen to occupy this ministry and apostleship from which Judas turned aside to go to his own place.' And they drew lots . . ."*
Acts 1:24-26

*"After there had been much debate, Peter stood up and said to them, 'Brothers, you **know** that in the early days God made a choice among you, that by my mouth the Gentiles should hear the word of the gospel and believe. And God, who **knows** the heart, testified to them giving them the Holy Spirit just as He also did to us; and He made no distinction between us and them, cleansing their hearts by faith.'"*
Acts 15:7-9

WHEN YOUR HEART CRIES

Day 19
Knower of the Heart

Every year, dozens of applicants pursue medical school with the hopes of becoming cardiovascular surgeons. Even after four years of college and several more in medical school, a long cardiovascular residency is required. Many will pursue this arduous course to learn all there is to know about the beating heart.

Today, we will be talking about another heart, one that determines the course of our lives but requires a different kind of surgeon.

Turn in your Bible and search your Greek lexicon for Acts 1:24-26. We are still mining the word "know." We find Peter, the disciples, and a company of men challenged as they are compelled by scripture to replace Judas, the betrayer, with another man. Only two men seemed to meet the qualifications.

In prayer, they ask for direction:
*"And they prayed and said, 'You, Lord, who **know** the hearts of all, show which one of these two you have chosen to occupy this ministry and apostleship from which Judas turned aside to go to his own place.' And they drew lots . . ."* (Acts 1:24-26).

Using your Greek lexicon, what Greek word is used for "know" in the verse? _____

Now turn in your Bible and search your Greek lexicon for Acts 15:7-9. These verses, referred to as the Jerusalem Council, are well known because this is where the debate over the salvation of Gentiles was to be settled.

*"After there had been much debate, Peter stood up and said to them, 'Brothers, you **know** that in the early days God made a choice among you, that by my mouth the Gentiles should hear the word of the gospel and believe. And God, who **knows** the heart, testified to them giving them the Holy Spirit just as He also did to us; and He made no distinction between us and them, cleansing their hearts by faith'"* (Acts 15:7-9).

Using your Greek lexicon, what Greek word is used for "know" in verse 7? _____

What about the word "know" in verse 8? _____

Peter uses the Greek word *epistamia*, meaning "putting the mind upon existing knowledge." Yet, in the very next verse, he uses a completely different word, the same as in Acts 1:24 we studied above. It is the word *kardiognostes*, meaning the "one who knows the heart." *Kardiognostes* is only used twice in the whole New Testament.

The Knower of the Heart intimately knows our hearts: our mind, will, and emotions. He, after all, uniquely created us, our *kardia*. We are who we are because of these attributes.

In these passages, we find that Peter yields his position to God, the Knower of the Heart. He is the great Heart Surgeon. God brings wholeness and healing to our inner man, first and foremost, through His Son, Jesus. Through faith in Christ, we find wholeness. As we submit our mind, will, and emotions to His authority, He directs our hearts. Ironically, this step– this choice to choose Christ as Savior–is the very decision that charts the course of our lives and our eternity.

If I were with you today, talking about your life and where you wanted to have it take you, I would first ask this: "Do you know (*ginosko*) Jesus, the Knower of Your Heart?" Quite frankly, knowing Him and yielding to

Him daily is the only way your mind, will, and emotions can be directed by Him. Perhaps you can attest that He is your Savior and the "Knower of Your Heart," yet you feel you are in the battle of your life. The truth is, you probably are.

You see, the enemy doesn't ultimately care about your marriage, your dreams, your children, or your ministry. He is out to steal your faith in the "Knower of the Heart." He will throw everything at you to see if something sticks in your mind, weakening your will and playing with your emotions. Ultimately, he knows that if he can minimize your faith and weaken you, those around you are more likely to fall.

Yet we can confidently lean into a God who identifies as the Heart-Knower. Even if circumstances are difficult and gut-wrenching, or we experience feelings of hopelessness, we can trust in God's very nature and character, the One who knows our hearts. So, if you need to call on Him today, cry on His shoulder, or collapse in His arms, feel free. He's got you. He loves you. He sent His only Son to die for you. The Knower of your Heart cares deeply for you. Trust in who He is.

There is no higher name than Your Name,
There is no higher word than Your Word,
There is no higher joy than the joy of knowing You,
There is no higher place than in Your outstretched, resting arms.

Something to consider:

If we believe the Lord has cleansed our hearts through faith, we can trust in our Father, the Knower of our Heart. As the One who knows your heart, what is your greatest need: comfort, unresolved grief, loneliness, shame, or something else?

_____

_____

Pray with me:
Lord, You are the great Knower of my heart. You are intimately acquainted with my ways, You hear my prayer and yes, You see my cries. And yet You don't determine me to be weak. Instead, You invite me to draw my heart close to Yours. Thank You for not just knowing my heart, but healing my heart. In You, I can rest.
In Jesus' Name, Amen.

Day 20
Training For the Long Haul

I strength train several days each week under the watchful eye of my coach. One thing I have learned from her is if you want to lift anything heavy–I mean *really* heavy–you have to stabilize your body first. Your complete focus and effort needs to be on that singular lift. Without stabilizing, the move will not be nearly as productive. That is the goal of productive training: training for the long haul.

You, my friends, have been doing just that in learning to mine the New Testament. You haven't been spoon-fed. You've done a lot of work. In return, you've learned how to take a passage of scripture and dig a little deeper. Just like strength training, you have established your ability to study the Bible. You've "stabilized" your study practices to "lift heavy."

While you have mined the word "know" through the entire New Testament, my guess is that you have a newfound confidence in studying God's Word. You can "lift heavier" than you did when you started.

I can't help but think of Paul and his relationship with young Timothy. Paul, aware that his days were numbered, knew what would be required of Timothy once he was gone. He'd have to carry out the heavy work of proclaiming the gospel of Jesus without him, not allowing the purity of the message to fall away. Paul left him with these exhortations:

"Nourish [yourself] on the words of the faith, of the sound doctrine which you have been following . . ." (1 Timothy 4:6).

"Discipline yourself for . . . godliness" (1 Timothy 4:7).
". . . fix our [your] hope on the living God . . ." (1 Timothy 4:10).
". . . in speech, conduct, love, faith, and purity, show yourself an example . . ." (1 Timothy 4:12).
". . . give attention to the public reading of Scripture, to exhortation, and teaching" (1 Timothy 4:13).
"Do not neglect the spiritual gift within you . . ." (1 Timothy 4:14).

These same practices enable us to live out our faith. They are some of the ways we "stabilize" our spiritual life to "lift heavy" in this challenging culture. As we apply them, we heal from hurts, gain a fresh vision for our lives, and are challenged to live out the call God has placed on each of us.

And we all have a call, a purpose in Christ.

We've learned that it is one thing to know (*oida*) these things, to know through seeing or perceiving. Yet, it is another to know (*ginosko or even epiginosko*) through ongoing personal experience.

On Day 1, I asked you to be patient with this process, and you have done just that. You have taken mining and made it a part of your Bible Study process. While I would have loved to sit with you each day and have coffee together, I trust you have connected with our Savior in a powerful new way. I pray that hope has been restored through His Word, and you have found fresh vision and affirmation of His call on your life.

Something to consider:
How has God opened His Word to you in a personal way? You might have already written this on a prior study day, but I believe the Lord wants to enhance, clarify, and broaden your understanding of His call, His plan, for your life._____

_____

_____

_____

_____

Pray with me:
Lord, my life belongs to You. Apart from You, I can do nothing. But in You, I can do all things through Christ who strengthens me. I continue to surrender my life to You.
In Jesus's Name, Amen.

> *"Now to Him who is able to keep you from stumbling and to make you stand in the presence of His glory, blameless with great joy, to the only God our Savior, through Jesus Christ our Lord, be glory, majesty, dominion, and authority, before all time and now and forever. Amen."*
> Jude 1:24-25

Until we meet again, thank you, friend; it has been an honor.

Jeanna

Bibliography

1. Anderson, Dr. Lynn. (1997) *They Smell Like Sheep*. New York: Howard Books.

2. Chisholm, Thomas. "Great is Thy Faithfulness" 1923.

3. The Discovery Bible Software, NASEC Dictionary. (2023) H.E.L.P.S. Ministries. Word Study: 1987/*epistamai*, lines 21-23. Accessed June, 2023.

Know – Ginosko 1097

Matt 6:3	Luke 7:39	John 5:42	John 15:18
Matt 7:23	Luke 8:10	John 6:15	John 16:3
Matt 9:30	Luke 8:17	John 6:69	John 16:19
Matt 10:26	Luke 8:46	John 7:17	John 17:3
Matt 12:7	Luke 9:11	John 7:26	John 17:7
Matt 12:15	Luke 10:11	John 7:27	John 17:8
Matt 12:33	Luke 10:22	John 7:49	
Matt 13:11	Luke 12:2	John 7:51	John 17:23
Matt 16:3	Luke 12:39	John 8:27	John 17:25
Matt 16:8	Luke 12:46	John 8:28	John 17:25
Matt 21:45	Luke 12:47	John 8:32	John 19:4
Matt 22:18	Luke 12:48	John 8:43	John 21:17
Matt 24:32	Luke 16:4	John 8:52	
Matt 24:39	Luke 16:15	John 8:55	Acts 1:7
Matt 24:43	Luke 18:34	John 10:6	Acts 2:36
Matt 24:50	Luke 19:15	John 10:14	Acts 8:30
Matt 25:24	Luke 19:42	John 10:14	Acts 9:24
Matt 26:10	Luke 19:44	John 10:15	Acts 17:13
	Luke 20:19	John 10:15	Acts 17:19
Mk 6:38	Luke 21:20	John 10:27	Acts 17:20
Mk 7:24	Luke 21:30	John 10:38	Acts 19:15
Mk 8:17	Luke 21:31	John 11:57	Acts 19:35
Mk 9:30	Luke 24:18	John 12:9	Acts 20:34
Mk 12:12	Luke 24:35	John 12:16	Acts 21:24
Mk 13:28		John 13:7	Acts 21:34
Mk 13:29	John 1:10	John 13:12	Acts 21:37
Mk 15:10	John 1:48	John 13:28	Acts 22:14
Mk 15:45	John 2:24	John 13:35	Acts 22:30
	John 2:25	John 14:9	Acts 23:6
Luke 1:18	John 3:10	John 14:17	Acts 23:28
Luke 1:34	John 4:1	John 14:17	Acts 24:11
Luke 2:43	John 4:53	John 14:20	
Luke 6:44	John 5:6	John 14:31	Rms 1:21

Rms 2:18	Phil 1:12	1John 4:2
Rms 3:17	Phil 2:19	1John 4:6
Rms 6:6	Phil 2:22	1John 4:6
Rms 7:1	Phil 3:10	1John 4:7
Rms7:7	Phil 4:5	1John 4:8
Rms 7:15		1John 4:13
Rms 10:19	Col 4:8	1John 4:16
Rms 11:34		1John 5:2
	1Thes 3:5	1John 5:20
1Cor 1:21		
1Cor 2:8	2Tim 1:18	2John 1:1
1Cor 4:19	2Tim 2:19	
1Cor 8:2	2Tim 3:1	Rev 2:17
1Cor 8:2		Rev 2:23
1Cor 8:3	Heb 3:10	Rev 2:24
1Cor 13:9	Heb 8:11	Rev 3:3
1Cor 13:12	Heb 10:34	Rev 3:9
1Cor 14:7	Heb 13:23	
1Cor 14:9		
	James 1:3	
2Cor 2:4	James 2:20	
2Cor 2:9	James 5:20	
2Cor 3:2		
2Cor 5:16	2Pet 1:20	
2Cor 5:21	2Pet 3:3	
2Cor 8:9		
2Cor 13:6	1John 2:3	
	1John 2:3	
Gal 2:9	1John 2:4	
Gal 3:7	1John 2:29	
Gal 4:9	1John 3:1	
Gal 4:9	1John 3:6	
	1John 3:16	
Eph 3:19	1John 3:19	
Eph 5:5	1John 3:20	
Eph 6:22	1John 3:24	

Know – Epiginosko 1921

Matt 7:16*	Rom 1:32
Matt 7:20*	
Matt 11:27*	1 Cor 13:12
Matt 11:27*	1 Cor 13:12
Matt 14:35	1 Cor 14:37
Matt 17:12*	1 Cor 16:18
Mark 2:8**	2 Cor 1:13
Mark 5:30**	2 Cor 1:13
Mark 6:33	2 Cor 1:14
Mark 6:54	2 Cor 6:9
	2 Cor 13:5
Luke 1:4	
Luke 1:22	Col 1:6
Luke 5:22**	
Luke 7:37	1 Tim 4:3
Luke 23:7	
Luke 24:16**	2 Pet 2:21
Luke 24:31**	2 Pet 2:21
Acts 3:10	*Jesus speaking
Acts 4:13	**Jesus perceiving or knowing
Acts 9:30	
Acts 12:14	
Acts 19:34	
Acts 22:24	
Acts 22:29	
ACTS 23:28	
Acts 24:8	
Acts 25:10	
Acts 27:39	
Acts 28:1	

Know - Oida 3609

Matt 6:8	Mark 12:15	Jn 2:9,9	Jn 15:21
Matt 6:32	Mark 12:24	Jn 3:2	Jn 16:18
Matt 7:11	Mark 13:32	Jn 3:8	Jn 16:30
Matt 9:4	Mark 13:33	Jn 3:11	Jn 18:2,4
Matt 9:6	Mark 13:35	Jn 4:22	Jn 19:10
Matt 12:25	Mark 14:68	Jn 4:32	Jn 19:28
Mat 15:12	Mark 14:71	Jn 4:42	Jn 19:35
Matt 20:22		Jn 5:13	Jn 20:2
Matt 20:25	Luke 2:49		Jn 20:9
Matt 21:27	Luke 4:34	Jn 5:32	Jn 20:13
Matt 22:16	Luke 4:41	Jn 6:6	Jn 20:14
Matt 22:29	Luke 5:24	Jn 6:61	Jn 21:4
Matt 24:36	Luke 8:53	Jn 6:64	Jn 21:12
Matt 24:42	Luke 9:33	Jn 6:69	Jn 21:15
Matt 24:43	Luke 9:47	Jn 8:14-20	Jn 21:16
Matt 25:12	Luke 11:13	Jn 8:31	Jn 21:17
Matt 25:13	Luke 11:17	Jn 8:55 (3)	Jn 21:24
Matt 26:2	Luke 12:30	Jn 9:12	Acts 2:22
Matt 26:70	Luke 12:39	Jn 9:19-34	Acts 2:30
Matt 26:72	Luke 12:56	Jn 10:4-5	Acts 3:16
Matt 28:5	Luke 13:25	Jn 11:22	Acts 3:17
	Luke 13:27	Jn 11:24	Acts 5:7
Mark 1:24	Luke 18:20	Jn 11:42	Acts 7:18
Mark 1:34	Luke 9:22	Jn 11:49	Acts 7:40
Mark 2:10	Luke 20:7	Jn 12:35	Acts 10:37
Mark 4:27	Luke 22:24	Jn 12:50	Acts 12:9
Mark 5:33	Luke 22:57	Jn 13:1-3	Acts 16:3
Mark 6:20	Luke 22:60	Jn 13:7	Acts 19:32
Mark 9:6	Luke 23:54	Jn 13:11	Acts 20:22
Mark 10:19		Jn 13:17	Acts 20:25
Mark 10:38	Jn 1:26	Jn 13:18	Acts 20:29
Mark 10:42	Jn 1:31	Jn 14:4-11	Acts 23:5
Mark 11:33	Jn 1:33	Jn 15:15	Acts 24:22

Acts 26:4	1 Cor 13:2	1 Thes 1:5	1 Pet 5:9
Acts 26:27	1Cor 14:11	1 Thes 2:1	
	1Cor 14:16	1 Thes 2:2	2 Pet 1:12
Rms 2:2	1Cor 15:58	1 Thes 2:5	2 Pet 1:14
Rms 3:19	1Cor 16:14	1 Thes 2:11	2 Pet 2:9
Rms 5:3		1 Thes 3:3	
Rms 6:9	2 Cor 1:7	1 Thes 3:4	1 Jn 2:11
Rms 6:16	2 Cor 4:14	1 Thes 4:2	1 Jn 2:20
Rms 7:7	2 Cor 5:1	1 Thes 4:4	1 Jn 2:21
Rms 7:14	2 Cor 5:6		1 Jn 2:29
Rms 8:22	2 Cor 5:11	2 Thes 1:8	1 Jn 3:2
Rms 8:26	2 Cor 9:2	2 Thes 2:6	1 Jn 3:5
Rms 8:27	2 Cr 11:11	2 Thes 3:7	1 Jn 3:14
Rms 8:28	2 Cor 12:2		1 Jn 3:15
Rms 11:2	2 Cor 12:3	1 Tim 1:8	1 Jn 5:18
Rms 13:11		1 Tim 3:5	1 Jn 5:19
Rms 14:14	Gal 2:16	1 Tim 3:15	1 Jn 5:20
Rms 15:29	Gal 4:8		
	Gal 4:13	2 Tim 1:12	3 Jn 1:12
1 Cor 1:16		2 Tim 2:23	
1 Cor 2:11	Eph 1:18	2 Tim 3:14	Jude 1:5
1 Cor 3:16	Eph 6:8	2 Tim 3:15	Jude 1:10
1 Cor 5:6	Eph 6:9		
1 Cor 6:2	Eph 6:21	Titus 1:16	Rev 2:2
1 Cor 6:3		Titus 3:11	Rev 2:9
1 Cor 6:9	Phil 1:16		Rev 2:13
1 Cor 6:15	Phil 1:25	Phile 1:21	Rev 2:17
1 Cor 6:16	Phil 4:12	Heb 8:11	Rev 2:19
1 Cor 6:19	Phil 4:15	Heb 12:17	Rev 3:1
1 Cor 7:16			Rev 3:8
1 Cor 8:1	Col 2:1	Jam 1:19	Rev 3:15
1 Cor 8:4	Col 3:24	Jam 3:1	Rev 7:14
1 Cor 9:13	Col 4:1	Jam 4:4	Rev 12:12
1 Cor 9:24	Col 4:6	Jam 4:17	Rev 19:12
1 Cor 11:3			
1 Cor 12:2	1 Thes 1:4	1 Pet 1:18	

 Jeanna Swann is a writer and speaker and has been honored to minister to women all over the country. However, it has been through life's challenging circumstances that God has used to deepen her own personal desire to know Him more. Her greatest hope is to lead other women who are called and chosen, possibly wounded and weary, to experience Him like never before.

Jeanna is a wife, mother, and grandmother living in DeLand, Florida. She holds a Master's Degree in Education and enjoys her days at the beach.

Connect with her at @calledtoknow or www.jeannaswann.com.

WHEN YOUR HEART CRIES

www.ingramcontent.com/pod-product-compliance
Lightning Source LLC
Chambersburg PA
CBHW070143080526
44586CB00015B/1813